WHITE GOD FACTOR

★ **VIJAI MAHESHWARI** ★

© Vijai Maheshwari 2010

All rights reserved. No reproduction, copy or transmission of this publication may be made without written permission.

No paragraph of this publication may be reproduced, copied or transmitted save with written permission or in accordance with the provisions of the

Copyright, Designs and Patents Act 1988, or under the terms of any licence permitting limited copying issued by the Copyright Licensing Agency, 90 Tottenham Court Road, London W1T 4LP.

Any person who does any unauthorised act in relation to this publication may be liable to criminal prosecution and civil claims for damages

The author has asserted his right to be identified as the author of this work in accordance with the Copyright, Designs and Patents Act 1988.

First published 2010 by Coptic Publishing

A version of this novel has been translated and published in Russian by Vagrius Publishing House.

A catalogue record for this book is available from the British Library.

Library of Congress Cataloging-in-Publication Data

Vijai Maheshwari, 1969-

White God Factor

Vijai Maheshwari.

ISBN 978-0-9558771-1-7

1. Fiction: Crime
2. Fiction: Romance - General
3. History: Europe - Russia & the Former Soviet Union

White God Factor is dedicated to my father, BL,
who had studied Russian in University and inspired
a childhood fascination with the Soviet Union.

May his soul rest in peace.

white god factor

Prologue	page 1
Gradient Zero	page 16
Minus Twenty Seven	page 30
Minus Twenty Four	page 45
Minus Twenty One	page 83
Minus Eighteen	page 96
Minus Fifteen	page 106
Minus Twelve	page 131
Minus Nine	page 145
Minus Six	page 174
Minus Three	page 182
The End of Zero	page 190

prologue

The past broke into Irina's life again with a message on the answering machine from her mother: bleep, bleep, distant, the voice choked. "Irichka," it said in Russian, "are you there? They are announcing on television that," a pause, a sniffle—she imagined her mother in that green-wallpapered kitchen in Saratov, too close to the radiator, the hem of her apron still wet from washing dishes, speaking nervously into the red telephone receiver—"you've been strangled outside a Moscow nightclub. No, Irichka, my little rabbit, tell me it's not true. You're in New York, aren't you? Call me back immediately, we're sick with worry."

Irina was a big girl, a model with large thighs which she had never cared to hide under loose frocks or dresses. Instead she wore tights under designer shirts unbuttoned at the top to expose her white and symmetrical clavicles. She was proud of her chest: narrow and translucent, the skin taut as a blini. It gave her a confidence that other models lacked, a brash sexuality and optimism which had gotten her far in New York.

She flexed her legs, brought one up and touched the toe with her index finger before switching on the gargantuan satellite TV which dominated her modernist apartment in the Trump Tower. It was news hour in Moscow, 7 pm—something about Chechnya again, she sighed, then a press conference with the ultra-nationalist politician Zhirinovsky and then, right there at the end, a little blurb. The announcer wasn't even interested; he didn't cluck as an American might, he blandly read out the facts. Such things were too common in Moscow to merit much attention. "Top model strangled outside Mausoleum nightclub," he said. There was a brief close-up of a crumpled girl with smudged hair, welts around her long neck and her mouth agape, supine against the steps of the Tretyakovskaya metro station. Then an older picture of her, smiling, her hair piled on top of her head, taken when she had become a finalist at the Elite Modeling Competition in Moscow two years ago. "Police are investigating the bizarre murder," he added. Click. Now we go to Sports.

It was hot in the room, so she threw open one of the large windows which fronted Fifth Avenue and leaned out so far that the sill pinched her navel. Down below there were yellow cabs moving downtown, a pink awning defaced by bird droppings, and other buildings with bright offices visible behind windows—movement so relentless it seemed absurd that she might be dead. Dead, dead, she repeated in Russian, the thought itself new. "Poor thing," she said aloud, pitying the girl who might have died for her indiscretions; it gave her a thrill, reflecting on the chain of events which must somehow have skirted her. I'm a survivor, she thought: look how I came here to America, alone, got set up. Her thighs were taut, tingling under her tights, little ripples of half-pain reminding her of the morning's aerobics at the gym. "Ooh, la, la," she sang, pirouetting around on one foot while glancing at her watch to check if she was late for her appointment. Indeed she was, and so hoping to call her mum from the street, she ran out of the door with a scarf thrown around her hair, babushka-style.

At the agency, the receptionist was curt. "Irina, Ellen's waiting to talk to you," she said, and went back to her typing. It was her pencil-thin Manolo Blahnik heels, she knew. Even here at Metropolitan there were some who thought them gauche. Ignoring her, she righted her chin, and strutted into the inner office, an elbow twisted to grasp her right buttock with her hand.

"Hi, Ellen," she said, rasping.

"Sit down, Irina."

"Oh, you've got some invites to the John Michel Jarre concert!"

"What happened in Moscow?"

"Moscow?" She looked up from the invitations. "Why? Some new models coming in?"

"Irina!" Ellen pursed her lips. "Your death was announced on TV, wasn't it?"

Irina scratched her sharp, bright nails against the white of her forearm and slid the marked arm across the desk. "So what? I'm still alive aren't I?"

"Can't argue with that." Ellen drummed her fingers against the glass desktop, staring out the window. "What was it about though? Do you have any idea?"

Irina bit her lower lip. "I'm hoping it's a case of mistaken identity, but I can't be sure."

"It's happened before. Last time we had problems with immigration. She had a twin sister, it turned out. You don't have anything like that, do you?" The model shook her head, and made to retrieve her passport from her bag, but Ellen intervened with a wave of her finger.

"You don't have to worry about that. That was different—the girl was an illegal. But you're got all the necessary papers. You're legit," she pointed out, and was about to remind the girl again of her debt to them, when the phone intruded on her thoughts.

"Jaani, hiii. No, I wasn't. It's just a small thing here at the office with one of the models. Can I ask you something about it?"

When she put down the receiver she was beaming. She breathed deep, brought her bony, manicured hands together at chest level and then clapped them together sharply.

"I'm so scatterbrained at times. Forgive me. I just had a brilliant idea. Why don't we use your supposed death to advance your career?" She fiddled with a gilt button of her champagne-colored Prada jacket. "We'll put together a press release and send it out to the entire fashion world. You'll get lots of publicity for free, write-ups in some of the downtown magazines like W or Paper. All you'll have to do is be lachrymose, wipe a few tears from your eyes and stare moodily at the camera. It'll work great. Don't you think?"

She leaned over and stroked Ira's arm in encouragement.

"But what about me?" asked Ira. "It's not over, is it? They might still come to get me. I see it as a warning to me." The thought of this possibility, which hadn't really crossed her mind before, made her slightly hysterical. "Can you at least get a police escort for the next few weeks? Russians don't joke for nothing."

"Oh please," said Ellen, making to stand up. "Don't be such a cry-baby. You live in Manhattan, in the Trump Tower. They're not going to come for you here. They'd never get past immigration. Remember, you're in America now, not in some dangerous Eastern European capital." She rolled her eyes. "I'm giving you the chance of a lifetime, and you can't see the forest for the trees."

"But they can come here, even. New York is not that safe. They can do whatever they want, even in America. Last year, for example …"

Ellen stood up, held her hand out. "Listen, Ira, go home and take a valium. We gave you a prescription, didn't we?" She fussed on her desk, picked up an invitation. "Here's a ticket for the show. We'll talk more this weekend."

Escaping the office, Irina fluttered around the reception area, eyes peeled for the first Russian girl she could see. When she found one, she grabbed her by the shoulders and babbled out her problem in rapid-fire

Russian. The other pushed her away gently and then ran a long-nailed finger down her cheeks. "Irina," she tittered, her little teeth bent backwards. "Chto delat? You think we don't know anything? Ask Godunev." The model leered at Irina. "You're still going out with him, aren't you?"

Outside, Irina dialed Yuri Salminsky, cursing at the clicks and silences as it connected across the oceans. When she heard that familiar long beep, so evocative of European phones, she broke into a big smile. Beeeep, Beeeep, it went, with no answer. "Bilyaet, fuck." She dialed her mother. Beeep, again, and then a Haallyo.

"Mom, mom it's me," she gushed. "Where's Yuri? Have you heard from him?"

"Yurochka" A long pause, and then her mother bawled into the receiver. "Ira, my little tadpole, I'm so scared, he's gone into hiding, I hear. The Georgians are after him."

"Is it for real?" she asked, but there was just a long sob which turned into a wail.

"What's going on? You should never have left." Hanging up, she chucked the phone into her Louis Vuitton handbag and cursed loudly. Out of the corner of her eye, she saw a woman point at her disapprovingly.

New York can be strange that way. It's not a city used to sympathizing with beautiful people—not even in the tabloids. It put others on edge, her near hysteria; she noticed that as she looked around the bus stop on Madison Avenue. Hi, I'm dead, she wanted to say, but she knew that the bearded man in the baseball jersey would then follow her across the street and offer her some cash. He was salivating almost, curious, too timorous to look her in the eyes, checking his watch to appear unobtrusive. The others also had this glazed expression, staring so hard they had to dim their eyes to appear nonchalant. It wasn't like that in Moscow, where beauty didn't seem so possessive. In America, the burden of her looks was sometimes oppressive. She wanted some old coot with no teeth to turn around and harangue her for screaming in public, some babushka who would brandish her walking stick at her and then offer her a muddied carrot. Not here. It was too studied a response, everyone afraid to expose their desire.

"Oh, fuck you all," she cried in Russian, and crossed the street into Starbucks.

I must call Godunev, she realized. He knows what's going on, and he wouldn't hang noodles around my ears. He's cruel but not evil. Godunev. She didn't even have to search her memory to dial his number. 2-3-2 she started, tapping her legs, moving a knee up and down involuntarily. He used to do that, she remembered, turned on at the thought of his hands against her neck. Irr, he would say, Irr, don't kiss Frogs, referring to some Frenchies she'd hung around with when they'd first met. And then he would rub her collar bone until she murmured. She pressed on, resolute, 1-5-4-1, and then beep. She thought he'd pick up.

He answered the phone with a swaggering "Da." He had just arrived at JFK and was waiting for his Brighton Beach contact to show up with the Hechler and Koch. But she hung up.

Starbucks has these counters against the windows facing the street with high stools nudged up beneath their flatness. Irina was so tall that even when she bent over with her face in her hands and the Frappucino pushed away, pedestrians could still ogle the hard lines of her bra pushing against the svelte black top. She sat there, comatose, spilt images messing up her mind.

Godunev. Places like Moscow couldn't exist without someone like him, she thought. It's just natural that he was omnipresent there, the smiling charming hipster who cut through all Gordian knots. No-one knew him really, except for her. Or did she, even after all that time? He was from Vladivostok, some said, spoke Mandarin, the bastard son of an admiral, who had been disgraced and sent to the camps for collaborating with the Chinese.

She never asked if that was true. Just didn't care anyway; people didn't talk about the past then. He resembled Ilya Lagutenko from the rock band Mumiy Troll, with his bright, translucent face, and his sensitivity, like those portraits of the Silver Age poets—Kuzmin, Kharitonov—all victims to an inner aesthetic turmoil which kept them young. But it didn't matter what he looked like when she lived in Moscow. He was around, he was the one who made things right. Quiet, perhaps; nothing like those brutes, the *biznismen*, who broke out in tears once you'd sucked the cum from their cocks. No, the girls said that he just lay there and listened to the church bells ring. Whatever happened, Godunev would solve the problem. You needed a visa for France; or the cops had caught you driving drunk; or some Mafioso had threatened to throw acid in your face. No problem. You just kissed Godunev, whined, joked, cooed on the phone, met him at the El Dorado bar, and acted as if you loved him. And it was all OK. Smaller things too—a club card for the Jazz Kafe, invitations to events, dacha parties, papers to smuggle cars into the country, drugs. Either he could help you or he knew someone who would.

She was his girlfriend after all, the center of his whirlwind. She remembered him just grinning, baring his teeth, and saying something about Russia. Quoting Tsvetaeva. The walls of the Kremlin are just that, walls, made of brick and plaster. Some believed he was gay, she thought, but she knew better than that.

Irina was just one of many in Moscow of the mid-90s, before she moved to New York; another provincial model eager to be loved by the right people. She was ambitious—not that the others weren't—but her ambition was tainted by the West. She got that from her mother, the local beauty queen of Saratov, who had married the Party boss, and then watched helplessly as he fucked his way through the Komsomol, the communist movement. "Be independent," Lyuba Dmitrieva had told her, and so she had wanted that, to become a model, a real one, with her own bank account; she wanted it much more than the others.

Not that she didn't hoover up the coke, or fuck the bandits who gave her Volvos, or dance all night at Mausoleum, or spit at models who tried to steal her dates. She was bad like all the others, but her mind was elsewhere, in New York, Paris, Milan, on the catwalks, joshing with Karl Lagerfeld and Calvin Klein. It made her smarter, perhaps, this burning ambition, forcing her to learn all the terms, to work on her walk, to study the magazines and hang out with foreigners, with the dull, bespectacled photographers who wanted to talk—about contracts, share splits, agencies—all that stuff, the boring nuts and bolts of her business. She listened and had a way of widening her eyes, of breathing through her mouth when enraptured. Some men found it charming—Godunev did. He mistook her ambition for intelligence, and so had stuck with her all those years in Moscow. Sometimes he just wanted to talk, about the world, about how different it was out there, in the West. He had been around. And she could be a good listener.

Slumped over the counter at Starbucks, she thought about that tense afternoon in Russia six months ago after they had returned from a visit to Saratov. She had an inkling—for the first time, she realized now—of just how different they really were. There they were in the El Dorado, picking at their *foie gras* and pretending to be civil while she flipped through the fashion magazines.

"This is just kitsch," she had said, scratching the glossy pages of *The Face*, "80s stuff. God, how I wish someone would capture what's inside, instead of just trying to shock."

It moved him somehow, her speech, even though a part of him must have known it was put on for effect.

"You want to change fashion, don't you?" he had prompted.

"Of course, Godunev," she had said. "I want to be a model, not just a party girl, like all the rest." She wrung her hands, pointing at the tinted windows. "This isn't real," she said, "what we're doing here. It's going to end sometime. And I don't want to stretch it out like the others." Her eyes met his as she held his hands in hers. "I'm glad, really, that I'm going to New York, even though I was sad at first."

"Let's go to the Pushkin," he had said impulsively.

"The what?"

"The Pushkin Museum. Just up the street. Where we went the first time when we met."

"Ah, the Pushkin. Is there something going on this afternoon?"

"No, nothing, just want to show you the Donatellos and Gibertis for the last time. You're leaving, after all. It's fun, isn't it, sometimes, just going to the museum? Haven't you ever done that?"

"Godunevichka," she said, smiling sadly. "There's so much to do. All the packing, the last-minute stuff, meeting friends. Can't we go when I come back?"

But she understood from his expression and so stood up, made a motion of putting glasses on her face, and stuck out her tongue. "Let's go then. Just for an hour. Just for you, little rabbit."

He must have been excited. He said something about Russia she remembered, about the soul and moments of spontaneity; and she had become pliant.

They walked there. That was unusual too, but it was spring and he sent the driver away. Past the Dom Na Naberezhnoi and across the Kameni Most, down Resslova, the spires of the Kremlin on their right. He took her hand in his, turned up the collar of his leather jacket. "We could be in Paris now," he said, watching the roller-bladers come careening down the ring road past a young girl reading a book at the bus stop. They stood in line with all the others, and then walked into the room. There were plaster casts of the great masters; the twins Castor and Pollux; the landscape painter, Turner. The narrow stairs led up into the main hall where Repin's portrait of Ivan the Terrible and his son looked across to the doors from the Cathedral in Florence. "My father took me here years ago," she said. "He was a fat bureaucrat, with whiskers and a thick neck. I hated him. 'This is Europe,' he had said. 'We don't need it.'"

Near a bier, a marble imitation of something in Naples, he brushed his lips against hers. She responded immediately, pushing herself against him, entwining her tongue with his. He knew at once it wasn't right, that she didn't see a thing, wasn't interested at all in what he saw. She was just like her father. Saratov came back to him in a hot flash: that bourgeois mother of hers with her dusty cabinets of cheap souvenirs, her correct demeanor and lack of humor, the way that at first she had been embarrassed about him. So he dragged her down the red-carpeted stairs of the museum, out into the open, where they grabbed a cab. When they got home, he fucked her hard from behind. When they were done, he lay on the bed, lit a cigarette and blew smoke rings into the air. "Kiss me, Irina," he had said, "not the Frogs, kiss me." He had turned around and pinched her navel. "You hear," he said, loud suddenly. "Kiss me, you cunt."

"You're a monster," she said, rolling away, and so he spat into her hair and turned her face back towards him and bit her lips. Flicked open a Swiss Army knife and ran it along the inside of her thigh. She just lay there, her skirt pulled up over her waist, cum all over it, looking tough, her fists clenched.

"Let me go," she whispered.

He was furious, bubbling with rage. Couldn't tell from where. "You tried to just go along all this time, didn't you?" he said.

"Pretend that everything was great between us. But it's not. You don't know me at all, that's the problem. Two years and you know nothing. You don't understand that it's not enough just to smile and to charm everyone. Even that I am an existentialist. A fucking existentialist. Fuck."

"Get out," he said. "Pack those things and get out. Go to your New York and become a model. One day I'll come and kill you there."

Boze Moi! She sprawled on the counter, experiencing the pain of that separation all over again. Why, why, she asked herself? His threat was real, she reasoned. He wanted the money in their joint bank account, it was that simple. He was never that stable, even among the mad Moscow crowd. The murder was a warning of his power over her, even here in New York. Alternatively, she admitted, it might be a sign that he was on her side. She couldn't decide. She was convinced though that New York wasn't as safe as Ellen thought, was just as porous as Russia. They come in, the Ukrainians, on flights from Moscow, do the deed, and then return to some godforsaken industrial town in Crimea. Fuck, fuck, fuck.

"Can I help you?" someone said. She looked up wearily at a man there in a baseball jersey, all muscles and grin. She about to mouth "Fuck off", as she often did on autopilot, but the bulge of his chest muscles stopped her. My own personal bodyguard, she thought, and so decided to put some smile into her diss.

"Fuck off," she said, but her face softened in welcome. "So what are you trying to do? You are trying to be the hero and comfort a damsel in distress? Who are you to offer me some help?"

"I'm sorry, but you looked like you might need some comfort." As he stammered the line out, she could tell it was his big experiment. I'm lucky, she reasoned—he's shown up just at the right moment. She lowered her eyelashes and allowed herself to blush.

"Perhaps I do. I've had a pretty rough day. I kinda had a near-death experience."

He laughed loudly, as Americans tend to when nervous. "That happens to me almost every day in this fucking city!" Then he held out his hand, which was surprisingly small for his frame.

"I'm Clarence."

"Irina," she said, squeezing his hand lightly.

"Interesting name. East European?"

"Do you know martial arts?" she replied.

"Why," said Clarence, mock-boxing. "How did you guess. I study Tai Kwan Do."

"Let's go then. Show me something."

He blushed red around the ears. "This isn't the place, is it? I mean, we're just getting acquainted."

"Oh, stop being so American. Come on, do a couple of turns, strut your stuff."

Looking around, he shrugged at the man behind the counter, and then turned around—hands balled into fists, legs stretched out—and banged his hand against the counter. Ha ki do, mane san, and he spun around again, right hand raised like the Statue of Liberty.

"That's enough," said Irina, holding up her hand. "Let's go."

"Go, go where?"

"To my place, moron. I like tough guys." Linking her hand in his, she led him out the door.

He's useful, she thought. He can help me should they come knocking tonight. He's strong. Plus, he's American. Killing an American creates problems.

It was another beautiful early fall day, just like that afternoon in Moscow with a lone girl sitting at a bus stop and the roller-bladers in their anoraks.

"You ever just go to the Guggenheim for fun?" she asked him.

"Are you a, a …." he began.

"A what?"

"I mean, I don't know. Listen, I like you and all, I think you're the sexiest thing I've ever met, but I'm not the kind of guy who does that kind of thing. I'm an accountant, just a normal guy. I like to play around, but it doesn't …"

"Oh, shut up." She reached across and ran her hand across his bald spot. "I'm a model.

"A dead one," she added in an undertone, but he didn't hear. "Here," she went, and pulled out her Metropolitan card. "That's me."

He squinted at it and pulled up his glasses. "Wow, a real model. That's cool. You're Russian, right?"

"Right. Well, let's take a cab," she suggested. Jumping into one, she pulled him into it.

He was nonplussed by her apartment, by its size and connotations of wealth. He just sat there near her coffee table and looked out at the view, unsure what to do next.

"Wow," he kept saying, "are you sure you want me here?"

"I want you to spend the night," said Irina, pulling off her top, and rubbing her breasts against his perspiring face. "I like you, you're cute. You're not as rough as Russian men."

"Come here," she said. Dragging him to the door, she asked him: "Could someone get in easily if they wanted to?"

He looked at the steel door, knocked his hands against it, and then put his right ear to the frame.

"No, you're as safe as Fort Knox here. This is the Trump Tower, isn't it? You don't have much to worry about."

"OK, ok, it's just an old boyfriend," she said. "Why don't you have a drink?"

They sat there, whiskeys in hand, and drank, looking out the window at New York. He didn't know quite how to act, but as he got drunker, he let his hand rest against her knees, rubbing it back and forth, even venturing as far as her inner thighs. She liked the shape of his muscles and deltoids; she thought of him protecting her, acting as a human shield when they walked through the door. So she smiled and charmed him and told him stories about her modeling career.

"How come you don't have a boyfriend?" he wanted to know. He kept asking that question, not discouraged by her shrugs.

"Because most men are assholes," she explained, "all these agents and photographers and businessmen, they just want sex. You can't talk to them about art, or Dostoevsky, or something like that, you know. I just see it as a career, a way to make some money and retire early. I never go to the parties, it's so shallow, all that stuff. The New York scene."

He nodded. He had a high-pitched voice, which came from having to think too much about what he said. "I understand," he confided, "I've lived in New York 15 years, and I've never gotten into that. The clubs and all the promoters. I prefer to just watch baseball and HBO, you know, go to rock clubs sometimes. Guns N' Roses are my favorite, when I'm in the mood to rock out and let my hair down. You got any of their albums here?"

"Perhaps we can do some coke," she suggested, pulling a compact from her bag and breaking some lines upon it.

"Coke!" His eyes widened. "I don't do that stuff."

"No, no, you'll feel better. It relaxes you. I've had a stressful day. My mother in Russia is sick. I might have to go back soon for a visit."

She had to push his head down to make him snort it, and then he went along, sucking it up slow. It was good stuff, she knew that, and she felt it focusing her ego, making it all-consuming, justifying the past. It didn't seem to have that effect upon him. He clenched and unclenched his fists, staring around him with suspicion.

"Are you sure you live here alone? This is a pretty big place for someone your age." He got up and hurriedly scoped out her pad, peeking into the bedroom and bathroom, but didn't seem any happier when he returned.

"I feel a bit strange, my heart's beating too fast, like a chicken in a cage. I should just get going – have to work tomorrow, after all."

"No," she objected, restraining him and sitting him forcefully on the chair. She was getting aggressive, as she often did when high or drunk. Putting some Carl Cox on the stereo, she slipped off her dress, and gyrated for his benefit. As the music built to a climax, she arched her back stripper-style and rotated her hips towards him. This was the point when most men grabbed her waist and started to work themselves into a frenzy, but he shied away. When she came even closer and brought her breasts against his face, he responded for a moment, pushing her bra aside to lick her nipples. But, he gave that up quickly, and stood up again to go.

"You're the sexiest women I've been with in a long, long time," he admitted, shaking his head in slight wonder. "But I feel weird, not used to this stuff. I gotta go get some fresh air."

"Sure," she said, relenting. "Whatever. The key's in the door."

Just as he made to leave though, the doorbell rang. Strange, she thought, becoming panicky. The doorman usually rings up beforehand when a guest arrives. Godunev?, she half-thought, but banished it from her mind instantly. It was just too incongruous a thought.

road to zero

When Salminsky confirmed one afternoon, after a long drinking bout, that he sought my help in privatizing the Kremlin, I should have walked up to him, stuck my tongue out so that it grazed his forehead, and skipped out of his apartment. But it was spring—more than two years since I had moved back to Moscow from New York—and I couldn't think right. The scaly puddles and slush of late winter had just been skimmed from the pavements; colors escaped from the palette and attached themselves to the facades, dun-blue and umber again; and daisies sprouted besides the roads outside Moscow in waving streaks of yellow. The beech trees were green once more—the leaves shot out suddenly last night. I had woken this morning to an effusion of greenery, and called out to Irina, "Look, look, everywhere leaves."

We had gamboled out of our building to the park near the river without even having brushed our teeth. Wandered in the grass carefree and were swept into a game of tag with a babushka's fox terrier. She begrudged us our pleasure, the harridan, calling the police sometimes when we threw parties. But this morning she had pulled a twig of mint from under her scarf and offered it to Irina. "For fertility," she cried. "The best babies are those conceived in the spring."

So instead I tapped my feet against the hardwood floors of Salminsky's pad and hid my fears under a smirk. A beam of light bouncing off the pool table highlighted his vodka-inflamed eyes, leaving the rest of his face in shadow. His lips curled in the light's penumbra and then broke into a smile, his eyes searchlights seeking me out. A hard and tiny knot of pressure in my gut dissolved into my back. It could have been far worse—for a while I feared we might even get taken out. When he snaked his hand out towards me I grasped it in mine and ran an errant finger down his wrist.

"What century do you want to privatize?"

"All centuries. From the Romanovs to the present."

I strode out of the living-room onto the balcony, beyond the brick walls of which you could glimpse the yellow of the Grand Kremlin Palace, squat and solid as an imperial guard.

I pointed. "That one, too?"

"No, not that. The Armory Museum, the Assumption and Archangel cathedrals, all the rest." He had that particular sheen to his face again, the one he used to get when he'd just killed or conned someone. He patted me on the cheek and then whirled around on the balcony, his arms splayed like a dervish.

"You know the Pamyat Azova Fabergé egg, the one made to commemorate Czar Nicholas II's voyage around the world? Or the Trans-Siberian railway egg, with its miniature platinum and gold train set? The cap of Monomakh, the traditional crown of the Czars. The priceless Madonna of Vladimir icon by Andrei Rublyev? All ours, ours. For 99 years at least."

"You've lost your mind. Of course I know that Russia's corrupt," I laughed, rubbing my forefinger and thumb together. "The Kremlin! Has your roof flown away or something? Too much cocaine?"

I was sweating, palms cold as ice. I could guess where this would lead—to extortion, to intrigue, even murder. I didn't need it, not the money, not the hassle. I'd kept clean until now—well, almost. Except for that money stashed away, that foolish dream of ours. It tied me down, kept me standing there, spitting out of his balcony, hoping he wouldn't come too close.

But he came up to me and pressed his fist against the side of my head. He was looking sharper these days, just a white Brioni T-shirt tucked under dirty Helmut Lang denim jeans. No more frills or silk shirts with scalloped collars or white jackets with gold cuffs. His hair was shorter, too—still curly, but combed low over his forehead. He might've been a playboy from Rimini if it weren't for the mad glint in his eyes.

"You know what the problem with you is? You lack imagination. Your mind is like a vinyl disc, very cool, but running along the same grooves. Parties, you can organize them." He held a finger up in the air. "And women too. You're almost part of the female sex, the way you seem to understand them. Probably you were a geisha in your previous life. You're from Vladivostok, aren't you? It's near Japan." He snorted and then brought his face close to mine. "Be more ambitious, think bigger. There are other secrets, too, huge possibilities. This is Russia now, where everything is possible, everyone can dig for gold. How long you think it'll last? Two years, five, six maybe. And then it'll be over, time to tighten the screws again. Are you getting me?"

He stood back, his hands in his pockets, and smirked. "What degree do you have?"

"I dropped out."

"Aah, understood. I was a mathematician, you remember. I have a Paul Erdos number of two. What was I talking about?"

"Fool's gold." We both stared at each other, eyes narrowed, arms akimbo, like those villains from Hindi movies in Soviet days. Raj Kapoor. Main awara hoon. He began a slow dance, just shaking his shoulders in the Georgian style, his eyes on me the whole while. Soon he twisted his pelvis, slow at first, just a grind, then faster, faster, until he was like Elvis, voguing on the balcony. Someone inside had put on Mumiy Troll's new album, and the words hit us both like an epiphany.

On the corner waits a maniac
He wants to spear us with a hook.
Utikaaaa aii Utikai

He swung his arms outwards as he twirled around, and I followed their trajectory. Everywhere Moscow. Glittering in the spring, the still Yauza obscured by a thin film of haze. The spires of the Assumption Cathedral were shining forth like beacons. Beyond the bridge, over behind him, the husk of the Christ the Savior Cathedral peeked out from between the hovering cranes. When I first came to Moscow, I used to swim in there, a lazy crawl, watching the girls glide beside me with their graceful breast strokes, their long white legs luminous underwater. Now it was going to be a church again.

I was scared, I realized, frightened in the way I got when I heard of someone being gunned down.

"Salminsky," I shouted, "what's troubling you? What do you want?" But he just shut his eyes and kept up the dance. I remembered the gendarme in Cannes last month with his starched burgundy trousers, gelled mustache and peaked cap. "Oligarhh," he had whispered to his mate when we stepped off the gangway of our yacht, pointing at Berezhovsky, squat, balding, out of place in his shiny pink windbreaker and Air Nikes. "Oligarhh," a little kid with a snotty nose and a croquet stick had yelled, as if it was the name of a famous actor. Berezhovsky had primped and squared his shoulders, gazing past them regally.

"Why not me?" Salminsky had asked urgently. "Why not me? I'm better dressed than he is. Why aren't they looking at me?"

That was the problem, wasn't it? He wanted to be known and respected by everyone, not just the CD seller in his dark hovel, or the vegetable woman at the Danilovsky market. Real respect came from the gendarme in Cannes, or the bus driver in Stuttgart, all of whom should know that he—Yuri Salminsky—was wealthy and had the ear of the President, Boris Nikolaevich himself. These filthy scum were all the same.

I had this fit of pure righteous indignation like I once had when I slouched home from the kiosk stoned, past the track-suited gangsters throwing dice on the Arbat. I'd comfort myself with the thought that they'd fry in Dante's inferno one day. And then I'd walk to the Pushkin and wander its hushed halls, going silly over a Donatello. "Truth," I'd whisper, and emerge smiling, pluck a marigold and bite its petals. Chew it until the bitterness dissolved.

And now, what did I want? I had these hazy visions of lazy mornings and wooden huts in the countryside, a sauna stoked and ready. I fought to recall the original inspiration but it was like some half-forgotten Alla Pugachova tune. It couldn't withstand the light and the fresh air of the Russian spring. Down there were hundreds of pretty girls in short skirts and knee-high boots wading through the slush, turning their lovely heads at a passing Mercedes. Next month was that bash in San Tropez for Aksana's birthday, when Shura would sing in the middle of the swimming-pool with fire-eaters besides him. That silk Gucci shirt – I'd look fabulous, especially with that Om pendant dangling on the exposed chest.

Yeah, I would, if I were still alive. I didn't want to get involved, that's all I knew. It was like a scream going off in my head.

I went up to Salminsky and shook him by the shoulders.

"What's the plan? How are we going to fuck the Kremlin up the ass?"

He giggled.

"I knew you'd come around in the end. Fine, I'll tell you. Even if you don't understand anything, just nod your head. You'll only hear this tale once." He dragged me to his study, where there was some chart paper against the wall. Got quite serious, put on his glasses and gave me a blank professorial look before starting.

"This is the area of the Kremlin complex," he said, drawing a huge red triangle with a marker. "Now, there's all kinds of wonders there: the Grand Kremlin Palace, the Czar Bell and Canon, the Assumption Cathedral, the Arsenal built by Peter the Great, the Palace of Facets. Some of it was constructed by Ivan the Terrible, other parts by the Romanovs, and even the Soviets put up a few of the more modern structures. We can't buy up the whole Kremlin, of course. Even Yeltsin's Russia is not that corrupt. A privatization on that scale would bring down the government. But the fact is that the entire Kremlin, with all the historic treasures, is worth at least $50 billion." He paused, looked up from under his glasses and motioned to someone behind me. I was suddenly aware that the son of a famous writer had slipped into the room unnoticed.

"But," he continued, increasingly excited, "there's an organization called GosKremVhod. What does it do? It co-ordinates the entrance fees for all the museums in the Kremlin. With the dual pricing system for foreigners and Russians in place, an average tourist pays about $40 just to take a tour of the Kremlin. Given that about 200,000 foreigners visit it every year, that's about—do your math, folks—$8 million a year. Plus another $2 million from the Russian tourists. Not bad, eh? I could wipe my ass with that. But where's the money going? Technically, it should be used for the upkeep of the museums, the grounds of the Kremlin and so on, and the rest should go to the state coffers. In practice, it's going into the pockets of the Presidential Administration. And where do you think they've got the funds from to build their monstrous dachas on the Rublevskoe Schosse? The Presidential Administration has been investing the cash in high-yielding Treasury bills, converting the result into dollars, and then paying them back in devalued roubles. A great scam, eh?"

He turned to me. "You're following, Godunev?"

I nodded. "Almost."

"OK, ok." He rubbed his hands together. I hadn't realized until then how intelligent he really was. It pissed me off.

"Now the government is on the verge of bankruptcy. They're spending so much just paying off the T-bills and their loans from the Soviet era that they're broke. Even a huge IMF loan isn't going to help. So the reformers have had the bright idea (he smiled condescendingly here) of selling this organization to the highest bidder. In theory, of course. In practice, there's only one bidder: us." He raised his hand in the air.

"How much?"

"That's not important. What you need to know is that this state organization has legal jurisdiction over most of the valuables in the Kremlin museums. By law, it can loan out any of these artifacts for a maximum of 99 years. Ninety-nine fucking years! How do you think the Soviets made money? They gave these pieces to private collectors for five, ten years for large sums of money. Icons by Rublyev, Fabergé eggs, bejeweled goblets used by Ivan the Terrible—all of them were in Switzerland or America during most of the Communist era. "Loaned" to private collectors. Some of them are still there. So when we get hold of this firm, we're gold. We just loan these priceless jewels to collectors over the world for a few million and then sit back. Simple. When they don't return them after a while, we use the power of the Russian government to create a huge scandal. Bulletproof."

"What're the scorpions in the ointment?" I asked.

He chuckled. "So clever. Of course there are scorpions. Piranhas even." Turning to the famous writer's son, Arkady, he blew into his fist. "We could all get blown away, for example. Just like that Georgian did. "Yes," he said in answer to my glance. "He had the same idea. But we found out soon enough."

The famous writer's son raised his hand. "Tell him about the fund."

Salminsky's features distorted: he sniffled, wrung his hands behind his back, and then relaxed. "Yes, some of the eventual profits will go towards helping our poor Russians in the other Soviet Republics. That's his idea."

He brightened up. "It's a good tactic in case the regime comes after us. We're helping Russians, after all. Not just stealing." He raised his arms in the air. "We're not just bandits, we're philanthropists. You know, this is a new word in Russian, philanthropist. Earlier, there wasn't even that concept. How could a Soviet citizen raised on kasha and sausage even dream of being like George Soros? But now every oligarch gives some black money to the Tretyakov Gallery and imagines he's Rockefeller. That's our Russian weakness. It'll also pass."

Arkady, the writer's son, scratched his butt and spat into a cup at his side. I trusted him, even though he wasn't like us. That's partly why I trusted him. Yeah, he wore baggy jeans, cuffed denims and played "ultimate frisbee" with expats on Sundays. He might even have taken the metro sometimes. Most of the time, however, he just slouched around and acted the hick while we strained to stoke the madness. It was growing up in Maine with the hillbillies that did it, I think—his father locked away, pounding out yet another masterpiece on his Remington.

That's all good, I thought then. He's not as trigger-happy as Abramovich and won't kill, so with him in the plot, I'm safer. These Yanks are more cautious and they play a bit more by the rules. But still ...

I remember once—after I'd given him a strong Michelin Man ecstasy straight from Amsterdam—he came up to me flushed and happy at the party. "You know what Mayakovsky once said?" he asked. "'My God is Speed.' That's how I feel tonight. My God is Speed." I invited him into the inner room where the teen models were fondling each other; he stood there shell-shocked, fingering a velvet curtain in his sweaty hands. I winked at him. Emboldened, he rushed up to a girl and pinched her hardened nipple. "Ouch," she cried in pain, and spat in his face. "Idiot, fool. Who do you think you are?"

He reeled backwards, his hands over his face, and then advanced upon me, shouting. "Get her out of here. We don't want sluts like her to spoil the mood at our parties. Do we? Answer me, Godunev. Do we?"

What mattered then, and still matters, is that Yeltsin respects his dad. The girl was thrown out, while he watched, his upper lip curled into a victorious sneer. I turned to him then.

"Does Berezhovsky know about this scheme?"

He threw a glance at Salminsky, who was staring out the window distracted. There was a silence so heavy that, involuntarily, I followed his gaze, realizing the sun had disappeared behind the clouds. The sky outside was now grayish-white and there was a chill in the air; winter peeked its head back through the windows. I brought my arms together, goose bumps prickling my fingers.

"Bilyaet!" she cursed. "What the fuck is going on here? Will someone please speak?"

Salminsky made a fussy motion with his hands, ran them along the chart paper. "OK, he doesn't know. He has his own Fabergé eggs. He doesn't need more." He was speaking very fast. "Anyway, they wouldn't let him near this. He's already lined his pockets." He was red in the face, his brows knitted. Arkady gave him another knowing nod and he regained his composure.

"He won't find out. It's all being done through offshore companies." He rubbed his hands together. "Officially, Pinocchio is going to buy the firm. Pinocchio of course is registered in the Isle of Man but owned by Zepeto, a Nauru-based company. Nauru is a small island in the Pacific Ocean. It's a firewall. Almost no-one can penetrate it. Zepeto is then owned by another firm registered in Cyprus, which is under trustee governance. The trustees are under oath not to disclose the identity of the owners. And the real owner is …" he paused, danced a little.

"Irina?" I asked.

He waved his arm. "No, we've used her before. That would get too suspicious. It's the Georgian who was killed, Eduard Chevchavadze.

Even if they track us down, all they get is a dead man. Even the trustees don't know he's been killed. They've met someone who looks like him and that's enough for them." He applauded himself. "Brilliant, isn't it? Pinocchio and a dead Georgian are going to own Russia's priceless treasures soon."

"How much?"

He frowned again, furrowed his brow. "You're sure you're in with us, Godunev? We've told you enough to have you slashed in the outhouse a hundred times if you open your mouth."

"What do I get?"

"What do you get? What do you get? Borscht and blinis. Fuck! You get Pinocchio's dick. Enough for you. You get the Annunciation Cathedral, my dear friend. It's got all the famous icons by the greatest icon master, Theophanes the Greek. The Virgin Mary, Christ Enthroned, St. John the Baptist. There's also the famous Archangel Michael by Rublyev. Give one to Irina if you like. Sell them to private collectors. You'll be dead in 99 years." He paused. Smiled. "At least I hope so. For your sake at least."

I leaned back, lit a Parliament Light. "I don't like icons. I prefer the Renaissance and early Baroque. How about the Pushkin?"

"That's not part of the Kremlin." He grinned. "But you can do a swap with them. I think they have a co-operative agreement." I had that same light-headed feeling as when they gave me stacks of Benjamins to throw that first party. I leaned over to Arkady and whispered "Smart Estonian boy" for no reason at all. I chuckled in a sly New Russian way.

"You've got balls, Salminsky. You've got balls as big as the Czar's Cannon."

But he didn't grin. He wiped some sweat off his brow. "There's one last thing. That's why you're here. Everything's right, but that wolf—Yeltsin's bodyguard—is dead against it. We've talked to him, of course. But he wants one last thing."

"What?"

He put his hand to his crotch and squeezed. "He wants to fuck Zara Wonder."

"And the Queen of England, too."

"This is serious. She's coming here in August for the launch of Russian Vogue. That's our chance to organize something."

"Why me?"

He came up to me and ran his hand along my cheek. "You're such a charmer with women. You get in there, perhaps with Fellacio's help, and," he said, banging his fist into his palm, "everything'll be smooth."

I raised a finger in the air. "No Fellacio. I can't stand that pervert. He's been muscling in on my turf for a long time. I'd like to see him fucked by Kirsanov."

"Use him. Play him like a balalaika. He's just a bit player. We'll take care of him later."

There was some justice in the idea of that brute with his Meatloaf sideburns and hairy thighs banging Zara Wonder. It gave me a thrill just thinking about it. Oh, I saw her once. At Planet Hollywood in Paris. She was with Chuck Norris and Sylvester Stallone and some other stars. Sitting regally in a ringed enclosure with bodyguards in earpieces all around her, flashguns going off in her face. The bitch. We'll show her what Russia is all about. We're still a superpower, aren't we? Here in our Moscow we can do whatever we like.

"I'll do it," I announced calmly. "No-one gets killed, though. Is that a promise?"

There was another long silence and then the phone rang. Arkady picked it up, listened for a while. Then he turned to us. "Mausoleum. Sasha Mamonov's birthday party. Let's go."

"Let's grab a kilo of black caviar from Astrakhan Volodya on the way," Salminsky said. "We'll smear it all over the young girls' asses." He shook me on the shoulder. "To celebrate our pact."

"Yes," I mumbled. "Let's go."

"No-one gets killed, right?" I asked again, when we were in the elevator. But Salminsky just massaged my shoulders and tittered. "Relax, Godunev. Just think of this as another excuse to party. You've been paid in advance, haven't you?"

It wasn't an easy decision—resolving to flatter their hubris. It's true that my hands were tied by the crime Irina and I had committed a year ago, diverting some of Salminsky's offshore funds to our Latvian bank account. If I had refused, I'd be a pariah, forced into exile and to wandering the world again. Even if I were rich this time, and could escape their wrath, I didn't have the stomach then for another dose of the West: it hadn't clicked with me.

I'd done numerous odd jobs in the four years I spent abroad. Some were legal: working in bars in Tel Aviv and on cruise ships in the Caribbean; selling used cars in Florida. Most, though, were illegal: insurance scams, falsifying medical records, hawking black market gasoline in Brighton Beach. Money had never been a problem—earning enough, that is, to get piss drunk on the weekends and to splurge Sundays on designer jeans. The problem is that I never could accept being marginalized, categorized as an immigrant and treated with condescension. I wasn't willing to wait a decade or more until that taint disappeared. Thus, being complicit in the outrage against Zara Wonder, the all-American girl, was a revenge against the humiliations I'd suffered, especially in America—a country which can't accept you until you've internalized its puerile pop culture; a country which manufactures mass insecurity so skillfully that everyone starts to question their every basic instinct. Outsiders like me who refuse to blend in and affirm its pre-eminence are then treated with suspicion, or incomprehension.

This is all just the tip of the iceberg, though. I'd lived so intensely in the six years since leaving Russia that it now seems like another life. I feel sometimes—like the rest of our circle—that I've been reincarnated since the Soviet empire collapsed.

There are some philosophers, Hegel among them, who defined time as the gap between intention and action. That's all fine and well in an ordered stable world. But what happens when action overtakes intention? When the equation is reversed, with events overwhelming society so completely that the world is transformed and all the old beliefs have as much use as a dated copy of Pravda? Mass psychosis and a dangerous gullibility are the results.

Time shot ahead so fast in the late 80s and early 90s that our wills were submerged. Most of us watched passively as the world changed and shifted to a new paradigm. When it was all over, almost no-one wanted to stay the same, except for those who thought the past would return. Even they though, were, like us, shell-shocked and bitter. We all molted and were forced to take on fiercer, harsher, less nostalgic selves, plunging headlong into the future. We were dazzled at first by Marlboros and Levis, imagining they'd compensate for the loss of our ideals. That branded panacea didn't last long, though. Either you left, like I did, or you ground your teeth and guzzled moonshine to stay sane.

There were exceptions to the rule. Savvy biznismen like Salminsky who kept in step with events, were preparing back in the old Soviet days for such a transformation. Most of these types—need it be said—were Jews. Their ancient culture proved more durable than that of Russians, whose minds were so dulled by seventy years of Communism that they couldn't adapt in time. Hah! So proud I am sometimes that I can boast a Jewish grandmother. Even the New Russians' imaginations were shaped by Soviet propaganda. Their genius went just so far in being the first to imitate its nemesis: the glittering, capitalist America.

Where did I take the turn which led me to Salminsky, to Irina, and to a world which believed so messianically in its own hedonism? To a universe which loathed its past so much for betraying it that its revenge was to deny both the future and the past, and to live solely in the present? To a Russia which had no patience for stability, or for the subtle messages of art or literature? When was my soul privatized in a rigged auction?

Let me begin at the beginning. More than six years ago (ancient history for us Russians), so that the present is made more intelligible. Years from now, there are some who might see our lives as part of some great historical continuum. But I'll be dead by then.

minus twenty seven

[Spring 1992]

I didn't believe in ambition. Nor in love in those days. But I did believe in perfect mornings. The sun slanting laterally through the open window, crosshatching patterns on a girl's tangled legs, reddish from the night's passion. Somewhere outside a bird twitters, a church bell gongs. You lie there inert, aglow, and then move languidly to stop the alarm's buzz. Ah, you think, this morning is never going to turn tail on us, and plunge back into the pillows. Later you sip coffee and stare at the wall, the two of you. Even the cracked wallpaper, pockmarked with the carcasses of cockroaches, seems aesthetic on that spring morning. Outside, there are sounds and rustlings; and even though you're hungover, your words slurred, you have the energy to smile at the others, pity their busy-ness on a day like this.

You can get addicted to such mornings. I did. They became a raison d'etre, a fulcrum upon which the rest of your life turns. Nothing else mattered except these moments of bliss. You start to plan your routine around them, leaving options open so that nothing comes between you and those mornings. In the beginning, it was as simple as turning down steady jobs, being condescending to friends who trudged to some bank or office when the sky turned white. Then you start to mock those who settle down, or who wake up to a baby's screams. Soon, you're a romantic, hair sprouting from your chin, your eyes larger, and dreamier, and your movements lackadaisical. It wasn't hard in the days when Russia was broke and despondent to turn into someone who roamed the Kursky Vokzal at night searching for a perfect morning.

She was that morning. I sensed it from the langour of her demanour, her calmness in the dirty hub-bub of the train station where I picked her up the week before. She had been sprawled on the floor waiting for a connecting train to Murmansk. Short skirt bunched up around her long, white legs; an arm perched daintily under her head. A few shots of vodka, a tour of Moscow at night, and there we were, sipping coffee in the kitchen with its green tablecloth. A big girl even then, with large thighs and a long neck, she wouldn't have been pretty if it weren't for her forehead. White and high, concave over the bridge of her nose, it grounded her face, highlighting her sensual lips and wide, darting eyes.

"You're not going to work today?" she asked.

I shook my head. "What about you? You take the train tomorrow?"

"My grandmother's waiting for me, she might be worried." She rushed out her words, slightly nervous as she formed them. "But I guess I can tell her the Moscow train came in late and I missed the connecting train." She'd been saying this for the past week, threatening to leave each morning for Murmansk. She looked at me again for encouragement, but I didn't respond. No point spoiling our accidental intimacy with too much enthusiasm.

"Let's smoke a joint then and take a walk around. The old ladies have all gone back home now."

She tried to laugh at my joke; tittered instead. I could tell she'd never smoked ganja before she met me, but I didn't want to make it easier. I packed the hash into the hollow of the Belamorkanal papirosi, twirled and pressed until the stem was long and firm, and then handed the joint to her to light. She looked at it, eyes wide, as she did that first time, and then took a quick drag as the flames burnt the paper at the end. Exhaled the smoke fast.

"No, not that way. Hold it in." I showed her, inhaling until my chest expanded, and then blowing out, the kitchen sweet as a bakery.

Ummn, she said, and then she was upon me, kneeling on the floor as she kissed me. Her lips were soft, warm to the touch, her eyes moist, tears trickling down as I held her close. "Oh no," I groaned, and then lifted her up, kissed her on the eyes.

"You don't have to. It's difficult the first few times." I took her hand and squeezed it hard.

She liked me. I don't know why. Just another Moscow bum, working a kiosk on the Arbat. A dark, cylindrical trap selling bootleg CDs, Snickers bars, vodka, condoms, and other sundries, with a narrow slat for customers. Most clients knew me as a pair of furtive, white hands, the long nail of my left pinkie painted purple for effect. But I guess I was still a big cheese for a provincial girl like her. It made me soft, her affection, so I sang to her. Just a little ditty. I was so stoned then I wanted sex again. So we went back to bed, not even bothering to draw the curtains.

This all happened years ago, seemingly in another century and in another country. When I look back now I wince. Not because of then but later. It was the reason I left Russia, I figure, wandering around for years—Tel Aviv, New York, Miami—working odd jobs, accreting contacts. It's also why I'm so rich now, so stuffed with dollars I could snap my fingers and some might think it means something important. Or perhaps not. I might have ended up here, staying at the kiosk, waiting for the right moment. Let's backtrack.

So we went to the Pushkin. It was the base of all perfect mornings, the glue which held them together, like church on Sundays. I took them all there and then made further decisions. Some didn't respond as they should and so I waved goodbye after we'd come back out into the light. The others, well the others. She was the others. She dug the Repin and the Donatellos, the hush of the velvet-covered stairs, the high ceilings with their motes of dust zig-zagging in the light from above. Even the babushkas: she gave them furtive, grateful smiles for waving us on. In her little schoolgirl way, she imagined this trip to be apt; it justified her unexpected stopover in Moscow. She opened her eyes wide as I explained things, made an effort to remember names and even stopped to read all the inscriptions. Ah, she said, at the Turners downstairs, we studied this in school. A bit provincial, her take on things, uncritical in its appreciation of high art, things placed in a museum. She was young, after all.

And then again, I wasn't a cynic then. Still a bit green, a bit patriotic, imagining the Bonnards and Matisses in the Impressionist chamber a political statement of sorts, some proof of Russia's cultural superiority. I hadn't been to the Louvre or the Prada then, nor the Met. So I squeezed her ass while she gazed at the Picassos and stifled a brief rush of emotion. Love! No, not yet. Beware, Godunev!

Outside she was scared of the cops. Crossed the street when she saw them approaching, fearful they might ask for her documents, her Moscow propiska. It was touching, the way this fear lived on in her as a remembrance of the Soviet past, and so I held her even closer, slipped an arm around her waist and kissed her hair as we walked past the Kremlin. Down through the Aleksandrovy Sad—all those ice-cream sellers—the great brick walls framing the greenery, closing us in as in a cloister.

"I was born here," I told her.

"Really?" Her eyes opened wide again.

"Yeah." It's an old yarn and I'd repeated it a hundred times but there was still some fun in the telling. "My parents were strolling just like this, twenty-five years ago, and then my mother had labor pains. And so right here, near the War Memorial, she went into the alcoves of the Kremlin walls and gave birth."

"No, really," I assured her when she blinked unbelieving. "It's on my passport. Birthplace: Kremlin." She rolled her eyes but she believed me this time like all the rest do.

"Where were you born?"

"Saratov!"

Saratov. Really. That's where my mother lived then. But I didn't tell her that.

"Yes, but how? In a hospital? Under water, like the fashion these days?"

She launched into a story about her mother, how brave she was, refusing pain killers and going in to work the next day. It was so patriotic, so shorn of irony, I was bored. It crept into the morning suddenly, this ennui, and I couldn't stand it. Sometimes I just excused myself and left them standing there, broke into a run after I was out of sight. Usually I disappeared. Just something to spice up the day, to prevent dishonesty seeping into the dialogue.

Go, I thought, but I couldn't. There was a part of me that wasn't so macho, that wasn't convinced that there'd be another girl like her waiting at the station next time. She's special, that side warned, much more attractive and smarter than the usual fare.

"What do you want to do?" I asked at last.

She snuggled closer, hadn't realized that the relationship had shifted in the past few minutes. Girls are intuitive, it's said, but not with men like me. We can hang noodles around their ears. I'd been doing it for years.

"Perhaps McDonald's," she suggested shyly. "I've heard they just opened on Pushkin Square. They say it's like entering America."

"McDonald's." God-damned provincial tart. But I liked that, I smiled foolishly, mouth agape, annoyed at myself for not being more turned off.

I guess we might, I was about to say, despite my misgivings, when that American showed up. Journalist or something like that. I knew him because he came to the kiosk, hung around and tried to impress me with bands he'd seen back in the States. Butthole Surfers, Frankie Goes to Hollywood, Dinosaur Jr., all those 80s rockers, so hip then. Wearing a rumpled flannel shirt, a backpack slung on his left shoulder, he came towards us with a goofy grin on his face.

"Privet!"

"Ciao!"

He extended his hand and I shook it. Irina nodded. He was impressed, I could tell that. Quick flicker over her short green skirt and breasts bunched under her unfashionable button-down white shirt. Alone as usual, always hanging around. I wondered what he did sometimes when the desire kept him awake at night. It's these Americans, they don't know how to get it up. Or so I thought. But still I was tickled that he was ogling her, making her even more precious then she was. We didn't value beauty in those days: it was just something that was around, like a hot chebyrek near the metro. Sometimes you slowed down and scooped it up. Other times you couldn't even bother to glance. This was before models, of course, before all those snotty agents started showing up in their flash cars, recruiting for the magazines and the shows.

"What are you up to?"

"I was just at Lenin's Mausoleum," he answered in decent enough Russian. "Never been there before. There was an old lady in the line who went down on her knees. Didn't realize he's still so popular."

Irina clicked her tongue. "In Saratov, we haven't taken the statue down. Some think it's all going to happen again." She composed her features, allowed a touch of false determination to mar her beauty. Sighed. "It's all past now. They're just living in their dreams."

I shrugged. I hated this kind of talk. "So are we going to get a drink or something like that?"

He looked around. "Sure. Here or somewhere else."

"Your decision."

"I hear there's this new sports bar that opened on the Arbat. First Western-style bar."

Irina tightened her grip on me, communicated her enthusiasm through those nails. "Sports bar. You pump weights and drink vodka at the same time. Some American invention."

"Nah, it's just a bar. I guess it'll be nice to watch American football sometimes. But otherwise, same old shit."

So we sat around a beech-wood table as spotless as the new rouble notes. The three of us, sipping frothy Western beer. Hinikin or something like that. Fat Americans in striped jerseys were playing baseball on the television. It was so strange. We were both intimidated even though we didn't want to be and it must have shown. I fidgeted a bit and couldn't be natural since I knew these beers cost more than I earned in a month. I couldn't get drunk since it felt like I was drinking gold. Fucking gold or diamonds. So I just sipped a bit while he went on about our prime minister, Yegor Gaidar. "Speaks like an American professor. 'Five hundred days and we'll be on our way to becoming a normal country,' he promised suavely. I liked him.

"He wasn't wearing a tie, just an open-necked shirt. He's the Prime Minister of the largest country in the world and I got an interview with him like that. Two hours we sat and chatted. Imagine that happening in America! This is why I'm here." He took a long gulp and smiled wide, his teeth so white I wanted to punch them in. Smiling came easily to these Americans.

Then he turned to Irina. He'd been avoiding her gaze, enthusing at me instead. He looked down shyly now as he asked her in bookish Russian. "So you must find this interesting, all this that's going on in Russia?"

"What is happening?" she asked, all innocent. I loved her then—It came back as an echo of the perfect morning. Lolling back, I stuck my tongue out at the sharp-dressed sportscaster on the television. Here I thought, there are cockroaches on the wall but we're still content and busy, not worrying our heads about nonsense. Free to treat time like a mistress.

Inspired, I ordered some chilled vodka from the waitress with the cheerleader skirt and bobby sox. It went down easily, bringing a flush back to the cheeks. I decided to go even further and ordered a steak sandwich. He was oblivious, just flashing out money when required, bent over in conversation.

"What is happening?" I remember him repeat in surprise, and then things began to whirl. Her legs had curled up against his under the table, her big toe poking out the sandal was just grazing his clodhopper boots. Damn fool, he moved his shoe so abruptly in response that it banged against the table's legs.

That's when I hatched the plan. Steal her jacket for her betrayal I thought. A revelation. I had done it before. So I casually stood up, mumbled some excuse about getting some fresh air, and walked out into the corridor. It hung there unguarded, a heavy fox fur, too warm for this time of the year. But then she was going to Murmansk, wasn't she? I ran my fingers through it and then slipped it on and marched out the door. Down the street and quick to the metro beneath which was seething with hustlers just like me: old men holding out tin cans of sardines, caviar black marketers, babushkas with socks or turtles cradled against their necks.

I stood there beside them in that feminine jacket with its ridiculous tear-drop tassels; a transvestite, for all someone might imagine. The air smelled of fish and excrement, the floor was black with slush, and a cold blast came out of the recesses of the underground when a train screeched to a halt. I thought it wouldn't be for long. Someone would come along, especially for a jacket like this. Must be worth about a thousand roubles at least, certainly enough for a train ticket to St. Petersburg and a night at the hotel on Nevsky Prospekt.

Champagne on ice, carriage rides down the avenues, stars bright in the heavens, a stray dog trotting along, sniffing at the horses' tails. "La Dolce Vita," I exhaled, but no-one came. Perhaps I was too effeminate—that has always been the problem. My transparent cheeks, smooth rounded face and full lips—they caused confusion. So I blew out of there some time later, slinging the unwanted coat over my shoulders, whistling a tune from that old Soviet classic, Brilliantni Ruki. The misadventure was funny, that's what I had wanted, and so I ran down the street, chasing a cat. I'll take Irina back and we'll make some blinis up and then watch a rerun on the television. Then we'll fuck again, I'll use the ikon one more time.

You have to understand. It's not that I was venial, just a small-time crook angling for some cash. I just acted on instinct, prided myself on a certain naturalism. Later, when we were all rich, it was an asset; others admired me, attempted in their weak, unimaginative ways to mime my actions and make them appear natural. The way I'd go out on a whim and take an old lady to the South of France, then get some magazine to write an article about it and later sue the publication for slander so that the editor backed down and praised our front company in Cyprus. It all worked out in the end. Then, and now. So I strode back in there without shame.

She wasn't there. He neither. I searched the bar, even the women's bathroom, but there was no sign of them. Just an ashtray overflowing with the butts of those cheap Apollo-Soyuz cigarettes which she smoked. Damn! I was so lost in that sterile futuristic bar I couldn't find words to express my shock. I went back to the table and picked a half-smoked cigarette from the pile, lit it and sat there nervously, thrusting my jaw out to shoot smoke rings into the air. It's not that I even wanted them back, I reasoned. A cup of tea at the squat. Misha could show me his latest painting. It took hold of me, this new purpose, so I made for the door, when one of those waitresses (can they really be Russians?) came over with a note.

She'd scrawled his address on it, such childish writing. And so many mistakes in such a short message. She must be dumb, I thought. We're waiting for you, it said at the end, the two dots over the Russian e left out. So I neatly filled in the gap and then headed out. A cup of tea, I thought, but instead found myself in the metro even though the squat was just down the road near Petrovka and the main police station. I'm going there, I realized, so I bought a bottle of vodka and took some swigs as the train pulled in. A foreigner in a bright rock-band T-shirt stared at me so I slunk into the next compartment. Alcohol makes me shy at times.

When I look back on that afternoon, it's not just her smug smile that I remember. The smile of someone who knows just a little bit more than you. Irina's good at that look, it gave her a cachet when she hung out with the Golden Youth. It's how I recognized her that second time as she sat in the fenced-off enclosure in the Golden Palace Casino; she had a little smile on her face when someone asked her to strip like the others pirouetting semi-naked on the small raised platform at the center of the stage. No, it said, and yes, perhaps later, just for you.

She was perched on one of those linen-covered Ikea couches which were so exotic then and smelled of the duty-free shop at Sheremetyevo. I remember my embarrassment, at how abashed I was by his hardwood floors, the minimalist décor and the VCR and Japanese stereo stacked up against a white wall. It was the first time I had seen a white wall that wasn't wallpapered in a Moscow apartment; and I almost shaded my eyes to shield myself from the glare.

"Hey, Godunev," he cheered, stretching out a hand. "Sorry about that. Irina was hungry and so we thought we'd catch up with you later. Glad you showed up. She was wondering about that coat of hers."

"Yeah, I got the note." They weren't fucking, that much was obvious. He was still much too nervous around her. Stupid American. When I got to know some I realized that they were all impotent in the brain, that they couldn't even express their simplest sexual needs without running them through a loop in their childish minds. But still, I couldn't look at Irina, who'd crossed her legs and was reading some magazine with glossy paper. Her silky hair fell over her left shoulder; and here, in this apartment, she looked like someone else, one of those Western girls whom I sometimes saw walking out of the airport with their duty free whiskey when I went out there to hustle for Marlboros. My hands were balled into fists and I didn't know what to do, so I smiled stupidly and walked out onto the balcony, Moscow bright around me, its seething desperation shining upwards like a curse.

Irina came out, whispered an apology, but even then I couldn't put my arm around her. There was a spot on my pants where some oil spilled that morning and I tried to hide it when I was back in the apartment. It felt like America, or least how I imagined America to be. I thought that if I spent a night here I'd wake up rich. I knew Irina believed that also—she couldn't even talk about the past there. Saratov, Murmansk: they were just swear words in this white-walled apartment.

So I took out the vodka and had another swig, feeling stupid, just sitting on the edge of that linen-covered couch, not daring to lean back. I didn't offer them any. I gulped it down and grinned at him. The screensaver on his computer, a Cheshire cat, smirked back. We all sit there grinning at each other. Even he seemed at a loss for words, as if my presence were an intrusion.

"Your girlfriend's very pretty," he said at last.

My eyes were now bloodshot. I glared at him and then at Irina, who was unsure how I was going to respond. She looked up from the magazine and shifted her weight away from me. How soon, I thought, she'd forgotten the perfect morning, and our blissful week together, her sitting there, so fragile, afraid to admit she'd never been stoned. And now this less-than-subtle rejection.

"She's not my girlfriend. Just friends. You can have her if you like."

It came out defensive and he knew it. But she didn't. Or she did and so acted to rectify the situation, bending over and kissing me on the cheek. An ambiguous kiss at best.

He protested. "No really," he said, "we're all just having a good time." He went to bring some more drinks. I followed him into the kitchen, hung around as he opened some wine, French or something like that; and having nothing else to do, peered into the fridge. There was a Big Mac wrapped in its package, sitting there on the middle shelf, incongruous among all those pickled jars of mushrooms and cabbage his landlady must have thrust upon him. It was so big and inviting, just a wrap away from a munch. Another new concept for me: ready-made food. I wanted it so I poked a hand in and took it out. He turned an inquisitive glance at me. Now I was embarrassed all over again. So I just forced a grin and pointed towards the living room. "For Irina," I explained, "she wanted to go to McDonald's." Before he could respond, I slunk out of there.

"Here," I said. "Here's a Big Mac. Are you hungry?"

She shook her head and then rolled her eyes ever so slightly. "We stopped at McDonald's on the way back." And then a girlish giggle, back to her old self for a moment, the words came gushing out. "I had two of them without even noticing. They were so good, the bread is the best part. So soft and chewy, isn't it?"

I bit my lip. "Yeah, well, I don't go there often. Perhaps Kirk wants some."

"No, you have it," he said, reappearing suddenly. "We brought it back for you."

"Oh, thanks." Now I couldn't refuse, so I unwrapped it carefully and bit into it. I'd never been there before and so was pleasantly surprised. The meat ground easily between the molars, the bread was soft and chewy. When I was done I burped, a slight heat and heaviness gluing me to the sofa now.

This damn Big Mac. It turned me into a patriot. "I see you don't have much Russian literature here," I said, pointing at his bookshelves, starting to rant. The usual shit. About Akhmatova and Isaiah Berlin, Mayakovsky, our poets, their great tradition, the richness of the Russian language.

I was so convincing that even Irina was moved. She sang Pushkin without warning—a stanza from Evgeny Onegin—her voice so pure and lilting, her face lifted up as if she were in a choir, the tip of her foot tapping out a silent rhythm. Her voice was captivating with its lulls and peaks, so was her white and high forehead, beads of sweat visible on its rim. We sat there transfixed and when she was done, her breasts heaving from the effort, cheeks blushing at our adulation, we both wanted to kiss her. He did because I looked at him and a question passed back, his mouth half-open. It was frightening, his passion, because he was so scared of it. He averted his gaze quickly and got up to change tracks.

I thought of asking her to leave when a tremor passed through my intestines. Bilyaet. Another semi-wave paralyzed me. It was an effort just to speak and appear normal. I wanted to get up quickly and rush to the bathroom but wouldn't. Why show him that I'm allergic to America. So cosseted here that a little Big Mac gave me the runs. A Russian boor through and through. Getting up with a colossal effort, I snaked a hand out. "Leaving," I croaked.

He didn't seem that surprised. Just came at me jovial. "Hey Godunev, we'll connect soon. Right! I'll come around and bring some more Jane's Addiction." For the first time I noticed that he was a big guy: tall and muscular, with shoulders which seemed padded. Face a bit square, as if hewn from stone. An American face. Not as distracting as a Slavic one, with a nose too wide, a nostril inflamed near the tip, hairs sprouting out one cocked ear. No, don't come near, I prayed, and he didn't, just walked past to unbolt the door.

"Godunev," cried Irina plaintively, and I wanted to be fooled, but I was too clever to be. She came to me, did the big Russian hug, mooned a bit, acted hurt, pouted her lips. Kissed me on the face forcefully and then gazed into my eyes.

"I'll come around later, be home, OK? Promise?"

I want to shit is all I could think so I just backed away, not even bothering with the usual courtesies. She must have thought I was in love with her; it gave her some satisfaction, my hurried departure.

Outside in the hall I couldn't wait for the lift. And when it came I jumped in, pressing the ground floor. Backed up against the walls and clenched my muscles, wincing at the pressure in my bowels. Another few seconds and I'd squat in the bushes. I didn't care at this point.

The lift stalled. First I thought it was a prank, that the two of them were just having a laugh. So I banged the door hard and hollered. But nothing happened. I rang the lift's bell and it gonged forlornly through the building. Doors opened somewhere, there were calls, and I knew it was just a matter of time before someone came around. This happened all the time here. I wasn't scared, not one of those weak claustrophobic types. But I couldn't hold it in. Not for so long.

When the pain became unbearable, I pulled down my pants and went down on my haunches. It helped that I was drunk, made it seem less pathetic. It was the smell which hurt most; the wetness less so. I closed my nostrils with one hand and propped myself up with the other, ogling the sticker of a Playboy bunny which was tacked onto the left wall. I guessed that the two of them would have started kissing, she keeping her lips closed as she had for the first few minutes of our first night. The Big Macs would be driving their lust. And I was stuck in a miserable lift, with the white sand beaches and the full tan breasts of the girl in the erotic poster rebuking me silently.

It was hard to believe in perfect mornings when some rich foreigner could affect you like this? I knew then that I would have to leave Russia, that I couldn't go on ignoring the cockroaches when the good things could suddenly turn as putrid as this. Russia, in that instant, lost its gloss for me. The picture beckoned, promising shinier and happier places elsewhere. Far away from this dump.

minus twenty four

[Winter 1996]

It's easier to get along with the bratva after you've been abroad for a while. Simpler to connect with their fierce hedonistic competitiveness, their mad desire to out-sex the West. Davai. Davai. Davai.

I'd watched them at Spy Bar and Pravda in New York, at Bandush and the Buddha Bar in Paris, flipping their fantasies inside-out until their imagination itself was fried brown and succulent, ready for the devouring. The weird thing is that I empathized even though I had nothing but an attitude that wouldn't disappear. Hair down to my shoulders, eyes bright with misplaced passion, I wandered the metropolises defiantly. Convinced, like them, that we Russians needed to remind the West of a joie de vivre that it had lost. Needed to help it recover the vitality which had sunk under the awful insecurity of the bourgeoisie. Call it the vestige of the superpower sickness.

So I flew back. Oh yes, I came back. Four years later. To Moskva! Glorious Moskva with its wide, dank boulevards and its lust for life and death. Wearing a loose kurta-ish white shirt, shades on my forehead, feet encased in wing-tipped Prada shoes, I step off the plane. Yes. It was just like those spring mornings—those perfects mornings when I didn't go to open the kiosk. The sight of the James Bond passport check women in their olive green tunics and gelled dirty-blonde hair is so reassuring that I blow them a kiss when I'm buzzed through the grease-stained turnstile. Even the stench of urine on the conveyor belt is as alluring as the cheap deodorant of Yalta's summer whores.

Outside it is just as I had remembered: Moskvitches and Ladas jostling for a fare, their vermin cabbies grabbing at my elbows. Cross-eyed, their faded leather bundas soggy with grime and smoke, their teeth brown and venial as street mongrels, the small-time hustlers come at me in a pack, pulling out damp sheets of printed paper which they waved before me.

"Sixty dollah. Just sixty dollah to centrum."

I am so sloshed that I veer and fall against one of them, my Samsonite suitcase banging against his knee-caps. He has four fingers on his left hand and a reddish rash under his left cheek. Not that I care—I just grab him around the neck and kiss him on the forehead, bursting out in Russian.

"I love you. You are the real Russian man. I really just love you."

He squints and blinks rapidly, expression verging on the hostile. Durak, I think. He doesn't understand a thing. I want to slap him, I realize, so I pat him on the cheeks. He gapes at me for a second—and then bursts into laughter when it hits home that I am drunk as a Siberian skunk.

"You Russian not American. For you $25."

"Davai," I say. "Davai."

"Kuda?"

"Nekuda. Prosto Centrum. I want to see the Kremlin. Afterwards we'll decide."

So we pile into the front of his sneezing Lada, knees bumping against the unstable glove compartment and our breath frosting up the windows. "Ah," I say, "this is a high."

He turns, unsure whether I'm joking or not. Handsome fellow despite the deformities, his sideburns short and hair well-kept and then—the eternal giveaway of the Russian—that firm, pursed mouth. "This is a high," I repeat, adding, "to be back after four years," and shaking an Apollo-Soyuz cigarette from his battered pack, bite the filter off.

That does the trick. After the usual preliminaries, his story comes pouring out. Injured in Chechnya during the attack on Guedermas, he had spent two years in a military hospital back home in the Urals and is now driving to feed the wife and kids. Classic tale, I guess, and in New York I might have spat out of the window and smiled at its amateurishness. But here it is more than plausible. I have missed the war, after all—what can I know? So we sit silent in that smoky cocoon, listening to the weather reports from across Russia—minus ten in Magnetagorsk, +5 in Yalta, -20 in Kogalim—I savoring the familiarity of those words and the blithe Californian insouciance with which the female announcer slides over the frigid scale. Even in Moscow, these places are a world away.

"Where are we going?" he asks again, swinging onto Leningradsky Prospekt, past the three musketeers—the high-rises near Vodni Stadion, a red Samsung sign emblazoned across them. I'd had a girl there once, a big loud divorcee who never left her apartment except to go shopping at the Produkti in the neighboring building. So long ago.

"To the synagogue! Near the library of foreign languages."

"Synagogue! Chto eta?" His eyes blaze, the mouth implacable in the light. I imagine him bristling behind a tank, eager to defend Mother Russia against nefarious foreign agents.

"Zoschenko? You know him. Trotsky, Kamenev, Zinoviev. They were all Jewish."

He just grunts. Forget it, I think. Give it up. Don't try lecturing a Russian. It has been a while I realize. I shrug and bite the filter off another cigarette.

"I just want to get rich."

He laughs, tension diffused. Changes into third gear and guns the accelerator so that the small car swerves in the snow.

"Da, that's true. Some of the Jews are doing well for themselves." He winks. "I wouldn't mind sitting around a table with them sometimes, sharing some zakuski."

Strange it must seem that I go straight to the synagogue upon arrival. Religious? (Vladimir Ilyich had done a similar thing too: Primo to the Revolutionary Committee upon disembarking from the Germans' bulletproof train.) You must realize that I'm not returning to take over the kiosk again, settle into the circadian rhythms of the past. This is an American mission: I have returned to forge a new identity, having arrived at the conclusion that it is only in Moscow that I might be able to do so. Not in Paris or New York, where we're still Russians, foreigners with an accent. How far can we go over there? Can we steal the Brooklyn Bridge or the White House as here we might the Kremlin?

So I haven't called the friends from those days. There aren't many of them anyway—I had been a loner while in Moscow, insulated from others by the singularity of my passion for young girls. And Mother! Well, she is still in Saratov, tending the dacha at weekends, reading tea leaves with her latest lover, and partaking in other esoteric rites with her hippie friends. A can of pickled mushrooms—Jewish mushrooms, yellow ones, known for never harboring worms—are awaiting my return. They are her favorite wild mushrooms because they make great flavorful soups! Saratov.

The synagogue is shut, boarded up; a line of yellow tape encircling its perimeter. The cab brushes up against it as it comes to a halt, its running engine breaking the silence. I peer through the frosted windshield at the crates piled upon each other in the yard and at the green construction mesh wrapped around its outer walls.

"Bomb blast," says the cabby smiling. "I forgot that I had heard about it on the radio." He pauses, lights a cigarette, the flame of his lighter so high it singes his eyebrows.

"The Jews must be protected by their God! In Chechnya, we didn't have such pretty clean-up jobs." He points at a block-lettered sign near its porticoed entrance. "No signs or warnings there. You stepped in the wrong place you got your balls blown off."

"Did anyone die?" I ask him quickly. Not that I care! Or do I, just a little bit? It's a reflex from having lived in the West: this overweening concern for human life.

He toots the horn. "Interfax said no, if you believe the news here.

"Shall we go now?"

"Where to?"

He turns to me and half-snorts. Something tells me he thinks me a sucker for having come right out here from the airport, from America, the land of milk and honey. To go straight and fraternize with the Jews. What a freak, he must be thinking. I'm almost overcome, on the verge of crinkling my face and apologizing in half-eaten words, disappearing into the seat as I do so. Sensing this, he shifts his bulk so that he's almost upon me and chuckles derisively, revving the engine at the same time.

"Kuda?"

"I don't know …" I am about to launch into an explanation when the arrogance returns, so suddenly it takes me by surprise. Fucker, I realize, the circuits connecting and synapses going pop! You are just vermin, a Russian peasant, while I have dollahs and have returned from America. Fuck you!

I slide my shades back into place and turn to face him.

"I can leave right now if you like, just walk out the car and not pay you a cent. You're going to go back to Sheremetyevo and get beaten up by your Krisha. $25, this is big money! I'll give you $30 if you like, even more, what does it matter to me, but you have to help me. You understand?

"Now listen to me. Tonight is Passover. It's like Jewish Easter, understood? I have a problem, I need to meet some rich Jews. Where can I find them?"

He blows into his fist, and glances back slyly. "How much are you going to give me?"

"Fifty dollah if you find them now."

He backs the car and starts to turn it around. "I know where to go. Dogs don't shit in Moscow without us cabbies knowing about it. Payecchali."

The Golden Palace casino is abuzz with activity. Black-tinted Mercs litter its entrance, guarded by tall men with braids on their tunics. I catch a glimpse of white, nylon-sheathed legs on the plush black leather inside a car. A moll shakes her luxuriant hair as she emerges, and then turns her back to me, the ends of her saber coat obscuring her legs. Then another Merc drives up and the process is repeated. Engine purring, a driver rolls down his window to stare quizzically at our snow-crusted Lada on the edge of the melee.

"What now?" asks Sergei, and jerks his thumb at the flashing lights near the entrance. "You're going to go in there!"

"Sure! Are you going to wait for me?"

He huffs. "I'm not here to attend your funeral."

I flatten my palms and hold them out before him. "Just wait. Here's $25," I say, pulling some bills out. "You'll get $25 more when I return. Park down the street over there. If I'm not back in two hours leave the baggage with the doorman. Otherwise I can always find you. Remember that."

Jumping out of the car I stride up to the bright-lit entrance where the neon silhouettes of semi-clad women flash exuberantly at me. A man steps out and slams his hand across my chest, barring the way.

"Invitation?"

I've done this before in Miami. I know the routine, but it's an effort not to drop my gaze from his insolent glare. Ex-KGB I think. Brute.

"Yuri Salminsky invited me. He should be there inside," I answer in English. It's the one name I have, the single card I might be able to use here. "A good man," Vasya had said the night before I left, bleary-eyed, staring into his tumbler. "A former classmate of mine. He was a mathematician once, a studious student even. Wanted to solve Fermat's Last Theorem. I could have been as rich as he is now if I hadn't emigrated. Thought I was doing the right thing leaving that garbage tip but then again. Go back, Vlad," he had said, tipping vodka onto the floor of his bar. "Go back before it's too late. There's still fortunes to be made out there. He'll help you, I'm sure."

The doorman squints and then stares back impassive. "Ne pani mayu. Chto ty choches?"

"Salminsky, Victor," I repeat again, and then continue in bad Russian. "He invited me. I have just come from New York."

He relaxes his grip. "Pakazi. Show."

"Show what?"

"Passport. New York stamp."

"Sure." I bring out the red Russian passport and flip through the pages until I come to the bluish exit stamp from JFK. "Here."

He brings it up close, stares at it and then sniffs, inhaling the smell. "New York. Klassna! Fantastic!"

Quickly, he shoves me inside, past the metal detectors and through the entrance. Fish—green and powder-blue—glide beneath the transparent plexiglas floor. Epicene women in black lace bras and hair tied back into severe buns, glitter around their eyes, are dealing behind the blackjack and roulette tables. A fat naked lamb rotates on a spit near the buffet table, laden with drinks and food. At the end, a large Star of David constructed from Christmas lights blinks at the gathering of men in tight dark suits, each of their Amazonian Russian women gripping tightly to black designer handbags.

Pushing through the crowd uncertainly, I look out for Yuri Salminsky. Black wavy hair high up on the forehead, Vasya had said. I grab a matzoh wafer from the table and stand around watching for an opening. Others are hugging each other: men with bowl cuts and sharp goatees glide around the room, faces bright and glistening. The Russian elite. I had never known the nomenklatura, the Kremlin insiders. They make me self-conscious, so I hunch my shoulders and avoid their inquisitive glances. I've got the Prada three-button jacket over the kurta and the velvet pants, but they're incongruous here. They're far ahead of the times, and, although I'm aware that I might use this look to advantage, right now it feels like a handicap. So I pour another champagne and turn the wafer around for want of something to do. Made in Belarus it says.

I expected him to be big and brawny, but he's squat instead, his black curled hair almost sprouting out of his ugly mug. Jeez, he's not a looker? Got a pinched nose, and wide lips that almost curl when he's silent. He's not the quiet type, though. I watch him through half-lidded eyes as he skips through the room as lightly as a ballerina, stopping here for a while, rocking on the balls of his feet, one hand pressed against his veiny forehead when a joke is cracked. Da, vapshe chuinya. Then he's off again, slipping through knots of revelers before he sights a new target. Sergei Artemevich, I hear him shout across the room as he half-trots towards his friend, hand outstretched in advance. When he comes close he stops suddenly, shakes the man's hand with vigor, and then throws his free arm around his shoulders, whispering something in his ear as he does so. Tiptoeing upwards so that he can reach the taller ones. Ha, ha, ha.

It's often quite effective, his crack that is. The other breaks out into New Russian laughter, nodding his head wisely as he bares his teeth.

Such skin they have! It shines copper-toned like the spires of an orthodox church. I rub my hand across the rough texture of my cheeks and cluck inwardly. I must stand out. It must be obvious that I'm not one of them. And sure enough it does seem that way for when Yuri Salminsky passes for the second time he gives me the briefest of nods and then breaks into a shout when he sights someone else behind me. Yuri Salminsky, I stammer, and he half-turns but then decides against it. The bastard!

What the hell am I doing here? In this perverse seder ritual? I'm not really Jewish!! Just hours ago I was … I was sober. Yes, that's right. Still, as the New York driver karoake-ed to Kiss FM, some Indian bloke. "Sir, I telling you, that, why you are going to Moscow? Cold, hah, brrrrrr. Heah, heah, there are no Communists there now?" In Central Park there were ice-skaters, joggers in shorts and padded T-shirts too, as we drove cross-town. I wanted to fuck. I remember that. The whole flight I had sat there languidly in the aisle seat, almost grazed a hand across the stewardess' buttock as she passed with her trays. It was a small, hard Novosibirsk butt. That's where she was from. It was because I was going to Russia. It had freed me up. In New York, riding the subway, I couldn't be bothered to risk opprobrium by raising my gaze to the girls, their pale hands gripped tight around the slippery railings, breasts askew under their polyester shirts.

I pour a champagne and gulp it down. And then another one. It doesn't matter anymore. I'm so drunk I stagger across the room and lean against the blackjack table, watching a bald man slice a carving knife through the abdomen of the roast lamb. He makes another incision to mark the apex of a triangle. With a horizontal thrust he breaks off a triangular slab and lowers it into his open mouth as others watch. "Sergei," a woman's voice admonishes. He spits, spewing chunks of meat across the white table. Hah! He turns around and cusses out a Twiggy-thin chick with fake eyelashes, and goes back to devouring the flesh.

I clap. Clap. Clap. I stumble over to him and put an arm around his shoulder. "Very tasty." He grins sly. He has gold teeth. He makes to spit again, stopping at the last second. "Boy," he says, "have some meat," and hands me the knife. I rip a slice off the lamb's right flank in one quick motion, so bloody that some of it squirts on my jacket. Yes. I swing the chunk of meat in the air and then its end into the champagne glass. Then I bring it to my mouth. "Russia," I want to shout. "You make my dick hard."

He comes up to me sudden and whispers quickly. "Who are you?"

I turn around and make a spitting motion. He doesn't even react. He just stands there, his smile frozen.

"Who are you?" he repeats.

I am Chang the Chinese acrobat and I have come to Moscow to learn some ancient Bashkyr dances. Flap, flap, I move my arms up and down. It would have been nice, wouldn't it? Instead, I shake his hand timorously, shake it a while more as I compose my features. He tightens his grip, squeezes the palm hard until it hurts so much I blurt out.

"Stop!"

"Who are you?" he asks.

"I'm, I'm a friend of Volodya Aksimovich. He said I might look you up in Moscow."

He doesn't even blink. Just rocks back and forth on his feet. A double-breasted suit I imagine would have gone down well with him. But he's wearing something too tight, a traditional Armani jacket and tapered trousers. His sideburns are so clean and regular they seem the work of some fashion designer. "The mathematician," he asks. "The one whose favorite prime number is 911?"

911! That explains the name of his bar. Really. I wish I had known that about good ol' Vasya. "911," I repeat relieved, growling out the numbers. "Of course. His bar in Brooklyn is called 911 too."

He laughs, through his nostrils this time, his suspicions zapped so suddenly that I feel like Aladdin with his lamp. "Vasya, vasya. That was a different time. Things were simpler then." He runs a hand across my kurta, twists the fabric between his fingers.

"So you lived in America for some time?"

"Three new years."

"Three new years!" He seems to digest the information. "Kruta. No, tell me," he says, putting his arm around me and gently turning me around. "What do you think of this place? Russian girls are the best, aren't they?"

"Nichivo! Not bad. The lambs aren't too bad either."

He turns at me and brandishes a finger in the air. "You're funny, you know. Friend of Vasya's, that's a bit mordant. What's the world coming to?

"Come," he says, motioning towards the other end of the room. "I have a small gift to welcome you to Russia."

As we enter the maze before the toilets, his face bursts into focus; eyes agog, his lips twitching, the nostrils of his thin nose dilated, he smells me. Sniffs me out for the fear or for the hidden reproof—as a hound or a drug dealer might. I'd recall that moment when the Kremlin sell-off brought the OMON to his residence. But for now I just slip a perspiring arm over his shiny jacket and smile a half-moon.

Hah, Vlad, hah, he says and waltzes to the bathroom. Ooh la la! Marble tiles, gilt on the edges of the urinals and that faint whiff of musk and after-shave. I sense the devil's dandruff emerging from his pockets and it makes me weak. I am perspiring even more in anticipation of the snort. Give it to me. Cut up a line. But he just preens before the mirrors as he brings the fingers of his right hand together theatrical. "Ruslan," he calls, when he reaches out his fingers. Ruslan? I swivel around and watch in surprise as this frail Georgian or perhaps Armenian man with an incongruous Stalin-like mustache and a bow tie emerges out of the shadows. Beria's former chauffeur, I learned later. He had driven the priapic Georgian murderer around Moscow in his armored ZiL limousine as they searched for chicks. Pulling them into the car and whisking them to a dacha in the outskirts somewhere.

"Davai Ruslan," Salminsky says, handing the man a small transparent packet. Ruslan's fingers I notice are long and white as swans' necks.

I say a lot of shit in the toilets. What else? Who am I at this time? Nikavo. A drifter from the streets. Vladivostok and the disgraced Russian admiral father emerge into the public space after the cocaine makes my eyes bulge. Saratov just seems too plain. Vladisvostok is more exotic. There are Jewish roots mentioned to account for the relative ease with which I had emigrated to the West. (It was having a Jewish grandmother which got me to Israel from where I left for the West.)

At one point Salminsky switches to English and fixes me with his excited glassy stare.

"You heard about the bombings at the synagogue?"

"Yeah, we drove past this evening."

"What do you think? Aaah, tell me, what do you think?"

When I express disapproval, he grabs me around the collar and whispers quickly.

"We did it." Why, I wonder?

"We Jews are supposed to be the salt in the soup. Without us there's no flavor, is there? What are Jews in this insane miracle of a nation? Cocaine in the papyrosi. White shit in the cigarettes. They make the dull Russians' heads spin. Prosto tak. We give them visions." He whines out his words, spitting into the air as he speaks. His English is impeccable, a slight American twang under the Russian chop-chop gunfire English, first syllables emphasized. He kisses his finger and rubs it behind my left ear.

Chop a line now, I sing. Cocaine decisions. You are the person with a snow job.

He straightens up. "What is this? Some American singer."

"Frank Zappa," I say. "The best thing about that evil empire. There's even a bust of him in Vilnius."

"Bust of a singer who sings about cocaine in Vilnius! That's pizdets." Something earnest comes over his face though, the cocaine perhaps having intensified his feelings. It is as if his bandit mask has dropped for a second and an earlier version of his operating system shines through. It is a collegiate face, earnest, seeking approval. "Sort of like Tom Waits, huh." And he smiles weakly, while awaiting my response.

"They're different." Now it is my turn. I chuck out my eyes, ball my hands into fists and throw them before his face as I whirl about the room. "Frank Zappa, he was pizdets. He was the cocaine in the Marlboro."

"Zappa with two p's?" he asks. I know then that I have him. I've glimpsed his craving, his desperate desire to be hip. Oh you poor rich boy, I think. You bandit bankir. I can hang noodles around your ears. I dance around some more and mock-punch him in the shoulder. Chop a line now. Cocaine decisions.

He tries to stare me in the face. "I lived in America also. Was a graduate student at Princeton for a year in number theory." He watches Ruslan chop up a line on the sink with a long-handled barber's knife, and shakes his head. Is there regret in his voice? I can't tell.

"That was another lifetime ago. I listened to Pink Floyd then."

The dervishes are whirling outside. A girl winks at me when I emerge and undulates her hips. I am moving so fast I think the floor is an escalator. Sweat pores down my forehead. Leaning against a blackjack table I watch the room carousel. There is some famous person singing on stage. Or at least I think he is famous. I must have seen him in a magazine somewhere. He has long disheveled locks of hair and a headdress of some sort. Mirrors in his caftan or whatever, plumes of birds in his turban, dangling earrings and rings. Transvestite gestures. The fat balding men sit with their tall girlfriends' hands in their laps and watch him beatifically, clapping on occasion. The other younger Russians with their smooth burnished faces and creased trousers are jiggling as he croons some maudlin tune, twitching one part of their body as if in Brownian motion. Later when I became hip to the Moscow scene I invented the Godunev method of jiggling about while standing absolutely still. I didn't move, not one muscle, just stood there apathetic at the glam nightclubs. But appeared to give the impression of motion or at least of partaking so completely in the mood of the moment that the feeling was inside. Deep in the soul perhaps. It didn't need to be expressed in the crudest terms. Others might jiggle around me and hug me as was the custom and I would stand there, still as the Buddha, looking enigmatic.

I see her first. She is sitting alone in the corner between a bank of faux-tropical plants and the stage. Hands wrapped around her black Gucci handbag, she is bent over a greenish cocktail, an expectant look on her face. Dressed all in black: a frilled skirt and a stretch black top over a white bra. Elegant, I guess, for the times.

I don't recognize her at first. I just want to run a finger down her high forehead and along the curve of her shoulders. The coke has turned me arrogant and brave. Horny too. But I am still nervous, unsure in the face of such beauty. Jittery, that is, until I smell her desire. Sniff it out as Salminsky had me. It is there in the tight embrace of her painted lips and in the slight flush which animates her cheeks. She is lonely, I sense, and she wants something. Something grand, something operatic, to shake her out of her ennui. Many Russian women I know are like that: too conditioned by society, desperate to be made whole through the intensity or the will of a strong man. The greater their beauty, the more their craving for intensity. Nothing like Americans, whose beauty is like a blemish one must learn to ignore if one wants to possess it.

When I reach her at last, I put both hands against the table and shake it so that her drink wobbles. Then I leer at her, eyes like stoned fireflies.

"Do you know it's a full moon tonight? I planned my trip so I'd return to Moscow on a full moon. You know Salome, Oscar Wilde. I heard the sound of wings beating on the way here. And now I know why."

"Oi, oi, what a romantic. You came to the wrong place, I'm not the girl you're looking for." Her hollowed cheeks are voluptuous in their inward dip, as if a skin-sensitive magnet were suspended between them. I notice her blush deepen so I move in closer, drawing up a chair and sitting down quick, grazing my knee against her bare legs.

"You're also a romantic. I see everything. Why are you here? All these people are freaks," I say, nodding at the gathering. "They all just love themselves. Let's get out of here. I have a small pod waiting outside. We'll fly to the moon and eat some blinis there."

She trembles without warning. "Who are you? Some kind of bankir?"

"Ja, bankir. I'm a taste-maker."

"Taste-maker? Chto eta?"

"You know clip-maker?" She nods. "He edits video clips, I edit taste."

"You're a maniac. A real maniac." But she doesn't resist when I enclose her small, long-nailed hand within mine. "Let's go. Here it's already boring. It's already morning. The angel of death has passed over us. We have nothing to fear."

She shakes her head slow, blushes again. "I can't. I'm working here."

"You're working?"

"Da," she says, suddenly aggressive, vowels dilated, last syllables thrashed out. "What, you didn't guess? You're not a Muscovite or something. You're probably from the moon. You have no idea what's going on here. Two hundred," she says quickly. "We'll go. That's a discount, just for you." She winks. "Because you're so sympathetic."

I watch the delicate, white skin crease together on her forehead. Flash. Flash. I imagine translucent cockroaches sheltering against its surface. Tears welling up in that delicate face. Irina. Irina, I suddenly realize. Sprawled against the cold floors waiting for her train to

Murmansk. Irina, I almost say. What happened? I wonder whether she remembers that perfect morning so many years ago, or the red-carpeted stairs of the Pushkin.

"A goldfish told me you had an American boyfriend. He dump you or what?"

She stares at me quietly, incomprehension struggling against some unexpressed fear. I cross my legs and light a cigarette. Stretch my lips out in a Roman smile. Wait for the memories to dispel the tension. She just grabs her bag though and stands up suddenly.

"You're a real maniac. How did you end up here?"

I rise too and bring my face close to her, so she can see the whites of my eyes. "You don't recognize me? Are you sure?"

She tries on a sarcastic, New Russian mask. "Perhaps from Highway Patrol on television. You just came out of prison or what?"

Remember the train station? Murmansk? Saratov? Raising my voice, I advance upon her and make the motion of slapping her. She raises the handbag in front of her face and jerks back scared. Others I notice have turned around and are watching our table. They aren't particularly concerned. Who cares about some tart in Russia? So I keep abusing her verbally until Salminsky comes up—still radiant, flapping his arms about.

I sit down when he arrives and take a sip from my glass of champagne.

"My woman's giving me trouble. She's getting some big ideas." I'm not afraid that Irina might tell the truth. She was too stunned, not sure whether I was part of the mob and might kill her later if she opened her mouth. So she just stands there, tears welling up in the hollow beneath her eyes. Circumspect, she smoothes her hair back into place. There is something girlish in the rhythm of her small hands. I loved her then.

Salminsky ttchh-ed. "Tch. Men! When are you going to learn? Every time we have a party something happens."

He opens his arms wide. "Well nothing to be ...," he says, before pausing in mid-sentence. A shoulder strap has come undone during the scuffle and the swell of her large left breast is highlighted against the black of her top. Such a vulnerable image – it brings back memories of my first love. The one who wanted to remember everything. We Russian men are inspired by violence, we wish when we stare upon its handiwork that we might emulate it, or even tame it. I sensed in that instant that he wanted her as much as I did. And like me, he didn't care about the consequences.

"Oh, what happened?" He rushes at her and pushes the strap back up. "You need to relax. I might be able to help you with a pain killer. You poor rabbit." And putting his arm gently around her (winking at me as he does so) he leads her towards the bathroom. "You stay here and rest. When she returns everything'll be normal again."

It wasn't just what I wanted but it was second-best. It was fate, it seemed, that every time I met Irina I led her to another man. There was a poetic quality about that, wasn't there? This had been poetic too. I was quite pleased with Godunev that evening—he had achieved quite a bit since arriving. "We're just friends but he gets quite excited sometimes," I imagine her telling Salminsky, when pressed about our relationship. That suits me just fine. Let him know me as the jealous friend until we meet again. And this time I have a sense she wouldn't be forgetting me. I'll be back quite soon, I decided as I handed the doorman a fiver before leaving.

Outside it was like a theater backstage. Drivers hung around the entrance, rubbing their hands to keep warm, the impressive Mercs and Mitsubishi Gallants disappearing under a fresh coat of snow. In the distance, beaming in the white winter landscape, was the faithful Lada, parked up on the curb. Good ol' Borya. He too might come in handy.

Tonight I'll check into the Hotel Ukraine. If all goes well, I'll have a perfect morning tomorrow.

I whistle again, remembering her face at that instant. That combination of fear and disgust. That's what it takes here in Moscow to get beneath the smooth burnished insouciance of the beau monde. A twist of violence.

Things don't turn out as I had expected. Do they ever? Just as we're pulling out, the girl dashes out of the casino coatless, waving her bare arms in the air. Can it be her? I can't believe it either for a second. But then. But of course. The world turns spherical at such instants. "Stop," I tell the driver.

Girls are so gorgeous when they've made up their minds. It might be something as silly as having fixed on a red dress in a shop window. But still, that moment of focused intention transforms their faces—gives them an intensity I want to steal with a kiss. That's just the way she is now. Her eyes dancing as she seeks me out. Dancing in the night. Ah, there! They narrow when they find me. She tiptoes a bit, breasts heaving, and then comes rushing at the Lada. Bangs her small fists against the hood. OK. I push down the window (the handle doesn't work), arch my eyebrows casually. "Yes?"

Without preamble, she sticks her head into the car. "Oh Godunev! I feel so bad. I offer apologies. I didn't realize it was you." She clucks, reaches out a tentative hand and strokes my hair. The cold of her palm is so soothing in that muggy Lada that I just close my eyes. "How many winters and summers it's been. I thought you became an American already. Kirk said …" At the mention of his name, I must have tensed, since she falters, brings her arms together and shivers. Then she fixes her big eyes on me again.

"Nothing. I'm just so glad to see you." Poor thing, I realize. She thinks I'm in love with her. That must explain everything. The sudden surge of anger. The hurried departure. It's nice though to be the object of such tenderness, so I bring a hand up and run it along her cheeks. She falls forward, closes her eyes when I press my lips against hers. I bite her playful, and she gasps, and then goes all soft, blowing on my tongue as I slide it into her mouth.

"It's so cold out here. Let's go somewhere else together," she says, her eyes bright, drinking me in unblinking.

"Why not?"

"Wait here a second. I'm coming back."

Halfway to the entrance she turns and runs back.

"Don't leave. Promise. I'll be quick." Kisses me quickly on the forehead.

Just then, though, Salminsky comes striding out of the casino. I see him first and nudge Irina, but he's found us already. Quickening his pace, he hurries towards her. "My little rabbit, what are you doing out here in the cold? You'll turn into frost. Here's your jacket." He holds it behind her so she can slip her arms into it. She smiles sweetly, and then turns back to me, a question mark on her face. "Let's just ..," I mouth when he nudges her aside.

"No, Vlad." He too pokes his head through the window. "You're a real Russian man. Proletariat. Where's your Mercedes?"

I just shrug. I want to insult him but I'm afraid. So I just raise the lever under the seat and push it back so I'm almost horizontal.

"I'm going. We'll see each other."

"Nyet." She shoves her hand into the car and grabs mine. "I'm coming with you. It's boring here. Let's go to Mausoleum."

"Let's all go together. My Mercedes is right here." He tries to put his arm around her but she pushes him away. "Yuri. You're a maniac. I'm going with him. We haven't seen each other for a long time."

"Mercedes is more comfortable." He clenches his jaws and stares straight ahead – sulking for an instant. I'm afraid this might turn nasty. But then his former poise returns.

"What difference does it make? Let's go together. I'll tell the driver to go home. He needs a rest as it is. Wait here."

Irina brings her face close to mine as we drive down Tverskaya. "It's so nice being among Russians again."

"I agree." I hold her tight as the car brakes to avoid something, and then, bending closer, kiss her on the ear. She colors, closes her eyes. "Mmm mmm," she murmurs. I go, "Umm Umm." She's still a spring chicken, I realize. Must be just 19 or 20 now. I sense her past loneliness in the tightness of her embrace and am protective. Rubbing her ears again I whisper, "what have you been doing all these years?"

"You know? I was a different person. I wanted to leave … Russia. I sometimes thought that I'd go to America and find you."

You were with Kirk, weren't you, I want to ask, but she sits up straight and gazes out the window at the approaching Statue of Pushkin.

"I love Moscow. I love the sound of the big city." And she pushes her head out the car and starts to sing, something from 80s Aquarium. Seconds later, though, she's back besides me, sniffling against my chest.

"Everything so difficult, everything so bloody difficult. Why like that?"

Girls I think. I wish they didn't make me weak.

She bites me on the neck, whispers, "I hate McDonalds," and then turns away to watch the passing arches. She sighs. Then she reaches a purple-nailed finger into her mouth and bites it hard. Memories come and go as gentle spasms on her face. I watch her as she falls inside her own looking glass, her eyes soft and bright as a rabbit's. "Irina," I whisper, but she snaps out of her trance, and, leaning forwards, taps Salminsky on the shoulder.

"Oie," she says brash. "I have a question. Men like you, do you have a club card for Mausoleum?"

I went home with her that night. What else? We were both homesick. I just for a large bed with clean sheets and four blank walls which shut out the world. She for a home. A place where she might wake in the morning and sing a little ditty while someone splashed water in the bathroom. A place where even potatoes turn into bizarre sex toys at some point.

Home. I remember the drive back. I can recall it all. After the statue of Gagarin, his giant ribbed arms thrust into space, we drove past blocks of grey and amorphous buildings. Birch and maple clustered around their barred windows, here and there opening into a little clearing where kiosks were open for a crowd of drunks. It was just like my first arrival in Moscow all those years ago. I had bussed in from the airport and stared at these edifices in the night, imagining that the whole city must be like this, a giant checkers set with squat panel buildings instead of round men. I feared then that if I clambered off the bus I would just disappear, be lost among those forsaken homes. When they found me I'd be crouched in a padjezd reciting Mayakovsky, a mangy black dog in my arms.

When I awake she is astride me, bent forwards so her hair brushes against mine. It smells of mint. Strange, isn't that, I think, and almost make a crack, before realizing I am back in Russia. No need to exert oneself more, focus even on making jokes during sex. Just lie back, watch the sun turn against the ceiling, and close your eyes again. I don't even bother thrusting, too much effort, just smiled when she began to pant and raised herself upwards, slamming down later. She slips a hand under my back and strokes my spine. "Relax," she says. "Why are you tense?"

I am, I realize. I fucking am. So I arch a foot, bend it backwards, and rub its sole against her lower back. When was the last time? I can't remember. I try to think back to Brooklyn, to that Puerto Rican girl who was into Jane's Addiction. A picture forms, we're jumping past a fire hydrant, and I have her lips, full, lonely, when the pressure begins to build, and it all goes blank. I start to thrust too, raising myself on my elbows; we're both in sync, faster, faster, me wondering at her aureole, so wide. Davai, I come. Explosive. I think she does too, not that I care. I'm sure she does cos she bends close and starts kissing me everywhere, her face moist, her lips mint-flavored. Godunev, she says. Oh Godunev. She doesn't get off me, though, crinkles her eyes second later, as she focuses her energies on squeezing everything out. "Ouch," I say.

She falls back on the bed and lights a cigarette quickly, one arm thrown over my chest. There's a second there when I might have been blissful, that is before I catch sight of the cheap Shiskin bear rug tacked up on the wall, and the faux Versace tablecloth, or the sad books stacked up against the white-painted dresser. The floor rug is as thick and hairy as a bathroom mat.

I want to leave. So I jump up and cast around for my Prada jacket and velvet pants. They're neatly folded up against a stained armchair, which smells musty. I grab them and start putting them on, check my watch. Noon already. Gosh. Well, I can check into a hotel and figure things out.

"Where you?" she asks, sitting up sudden. "Why?" Her voice is tender, not like last night's New Russian pose.

I drop my hands to my sides, shrug. I know I'm sexy without a shirt. "Just like that. Have some business."

"Understood." She lies back down and watches me behind lidded eyes. "Russian men, you're all the same."

I draw back the curtains and stare out past the cluttered balcony at grayish and naked birch trees, and the concrete stub of a high-rise in the distance. Moscow. I wish there was a line here, just one, so I could start the day right. Walk out of there and kick the bark of a tree, whistle a Victor Tsoi tune. Water the flowers, water them now.

She's upon me, little hands around my neck. "Listen Godunev," she trills. "I must tell you something." When I turn around she skips back and reclines against that horrible armchair, fishing in the pockets of her jacket. "Listen," she says again, pulling something green out. "I have a thousand dollars." Rolls her eyes. "Let's spend it today. This is your first day back in Russia. Let's go crazy."

"Show me the money." I count it. Ten Benjamins. Well, that changes things somewhat. I see the line against a silvered mirror, Ruslan's hands hovering above it. But wait.

"Where did you get it?"

She pouts. "Won't tell. Why you want to know?"

I go up to her and put a hand on her crotch, rubbing her clit through her black lace panties. I gaze into her eyes. "We're friends aren't we? Should there be secrets between us?"

She just closes her eyes and thrusts against my palm, going all languid. I remember again what a gorgeous forehead she has, so I move to kiss it, when she says sudden, her lips barely moving. "Yuri gave it to me."

"He did? When?"

"Last night, when we were in the bathroom. Just a gift he said."

I throw my head back and burst out laughing. I like that schmuck now, I do. I just imagine him, high, close against her in the stalls, his hand moving up her skirt. It gives me a kick, the idea of burning his cash while he waits for her to call.

I raise my arms high in the air, palms outwards, and bring them down quick against the bear rug, tearing it off the wall.

"Davai. Davai."

"First we find some coke and then we go bananas."

I tell you something: the foreigners are our enemies. Irina's the first to understand that. "Speculators," she says when I ask her about Kirk. "Stingy bastards." But they don't get that. The Russians, that is. Not yet at least. They still think the white gods of the West can walk on water, perform magic tricks like producing real dollars with their ATM cards.

Moscow is a playground for them, a freebie, think Russians like our cabby, who arches his eyebrows at our American accent. (We have decided to speak English during our jaunt. Will get us some respect, we think.)

"Yugoo Zapaedneayea," we say when we get into the cab. "Patrice Lumumba University."

"Americans?" he asks.

"Yeah," says Irina, continuing in bad Russian, "we're from Wisconsin."

"Americans!" He whistles. Shakes his head. "Fifty dollars," he announces sudden, without blinking. "Is that OK?"

"Fifty! Why just fifty?" asks Irina, feigning shock. "We heard that life is difficult for you Russians. How about a hundred?"

He's a young guy with a mustache and a sausage-colored knee-length leather bunda wrapped around him. "Hundred dollars? That's very fine," he says in English, and turning around, puts a hand out. "I'm Vasya," he says. "How about you all?"

Throwing the Lada into third, he guns it down the boulevard, skidding past trucks, tooting his horn when stuck behind a plodding Volga or Moskvitch. "I tell you, these Moscow roads, not like in America, heh? I come one day to America, and I become rich also. How much taxi driver make in New York? My friend tell me $10,000 a month."

Irina grabs my arm. "Tell him to stop," she whispers in Russian, so I lean over to the front. "Slow down," I say, there's no hurry."

"Yes, yes," he answers, "I will, I just show you some Russian driving first. You no worry. I driving car for fifteen years. I know roads here." He speeds up again, and comes racing up the incline towards the Lenin Library, overtaking a Mercedes to get into the middle lane. The Merc almost hits him from behind, and then edges past quick, a pony-tailed man inside giving him the finger through tinted windows. "You see Muscovites, bad people," screams Vasya, and goes after them in chase.

He's manic, revved up, talking as fast as he's driving. I don't care. I think it's pizdets—what the hell! But Irina's whimpering almost, her head against mine. "Give him the hundred and let's get out," she suggests.

At Bolshaya Polyanka though, he's going so fast, he runs through a red light, and then almost hits someone exiting a tram. In seconds, a GAI car draws up, blocking his way.

He wipes his brow. "Moscow," he says, "always some trouble. They don't look when they're walking."

When the GAI comes out, Kalashnikov in his belt, demanding documents, we skip. "Wait," he shouts turning back. "Just give me $50. That'll be OK."

But we slam the door and run away, jumping over the puddles in the snow.

"We should have given him the hundred," says Irina, when we're settled in the Mujaheddin café near the university.

"Why? He was cheating us."

"I don't know. We promised him, didn't we?"

You're a bimbo, I think. A bubblehead.

The Nigerian thinks I'm some rich Yank and that Irina's Russian. He's not that stupid.

"$150 for one gram," he says, and licks his lips, staring at Irina lasciviously. He's got a ring through his lower lip; his hair's dyed blonde. I guess he thinks he looks like Dennis Rodman. Freak. We should have gone somewhere else, but it's the place she knows. Later I'd find the gorgeous dealers who'd deliver the shit to your apartment and blow you for a few free lines. But that was later. Now, I just want it so we can start the day.

"Fine, fine. How long?"

"Ten minutes, fifteen maximum." He barks an order in some language at another black man working behind the bar, and then turns to us again, all smiles. His teeth are very white. Irina he likes. He's decided that. He puts his upturned palm near hers and quizzes her about clubs. "I see you somewhere before. I think in Chance."

"No, not Chance."

"Then it was Molotov Cock. That crazy place, I do dancing there sometimes. No, I not gay, just for money."

"How about Propaganda? Trety Put? Titanic?"

This man gets a lot of sex. That much is obvious. It's fascinating really, watching him. I haven't seen men like him in a while: American men are so tentative, well-behaved, their baser desires tucked away somewhere, left behind at the door with their bicycles.

I slip a hand under the table and massage Irina's thigh, grinning debonair at the same time. He knows what's up, but he doesn't seem to care. I get the sense he doesn't respect me. Some rich whitey he thinks. Doesn't get what sluts Russian girls are.

When the stuff arrives, he insists on doing a line with us in the bathroom. Just one, he says, for the favor, and grins again, his teeth so white. Irina turns to me, a question in her face. Fuck. This is going too far. The prick. I pull out a mobile from my pocket, and pretend to dial.

"Who's your Krisha?" I ask him.

"Krisha? What Krisha? Why you want to know?" But he's worried, keeps glancing at the mobile as if it's a pistol. "Who you call?" he asks, winking at Irina, flexing his exposed muscles. "We know everyone here."

When I put the phone to my ear, though, he stands up quick. Does an Indian namaste. "Listen boss, we friends right. No trouble here. We no want people coming. You have stuff, that good." And turning on his heels, he saunters out of there, banging the door behind him.

At the Versace store, I've decided the best modus operandi is to speak English into the mobile, and Russian to everyone else. It kills two birds with one stone. You lay claim to both the White God, and the New Russian factor. You are a New Russian White God.

When we arrive, the tall drunk proprietor, in a checkered plastic jacket, a little dog in his arms, comes running up to us.

"Whatever you want that's glamorous, lavish, it's here," he says, twirling his hand in the air. "Masha, show them around. We've just got the new fall collection from the Milan shows. You'll love it."

Irina's manic. She rushes from side to side, gushing at the sequined gowns with big silver buttons, running her hands across the bright leather minis.

"Too expensive," she says at last, coming up to me. "Even the boots are $800. I want the best or nothing at all."

So we fly out of there into the late afternoon where the hawkers are selling warm chebyreks near the metro and snow-encrusted magazines are laid out against benches. There's a music store around here, I remember, lots of classics. "Let's go there," I suggest.

The coke's made her desperate, though, mad for glamour, excitement and joie de vivre. Throwing a hand out, she jumps into the car when it stops, shouting "Maxim's" breathlessly and pulling my hand under her skirt. "Oh Godunev, let's have some champagne, some foie gras, and pretend we're in Paris."

The doorman at Maxim's—gold-tasseled uniform, shaven-headed—hesitates for a second, turning inflexible until I chuckle "See you at the Kremlin Ball this evening" into the phone. Hearing English, he's all servile, helping Irina with her coat, pointing graciously towards the main dining room. We walk in there, stunned by its wainscoted interior, chandeliers pointing down, glowing silverware set against varnished tables.

I want everything, whispers Irina; quiet seconds later though, after she's scanned the menu. The most expensive champagne, Krug's Clos du Mesnil, is $1650.

So we're out on the street again, at a loss for words. The Kremlin spire near Manezh mocks us with its glowing jade star.

"Let's just go to Starlite and get drunk," she suggests. So we pile into another car and head up Tverskaya, past the McDonald's on Pushkin Square, getting off at Mayakovskaya, running under the underpass to reach the diner. It's full, Tom Waits on the jukebox, the waitresses in pleated cheerleader skirts. We ease into a red vinyl booth and try to sit still, playing with the salt shakers instead.

"Baileys," cries Irina, clapping her hands. "Double Baileys with ice."

A few drinks later, we come down to earth. My hands stop shaking and Irina is quieter, shoring up energy for another upswing. She stares out the window at the white park, the benches thrusting out of the snow like scabs. "Soon it'll be spring," she says. "And you know what I want to do then. I want to go horse riding in Bitsovsky Park. I used to ride back in Saratov. We'll get a mare with a cute black spot across his snout and gambol him through the woods. Oh, Godunev, I can't wait."

She's flushed, her cheeks pink and her forehead twitching to the pulse of a thin blue vein beneath the skin. I can't help smiling. I feel so lazy now, can't make decisions. Perhaps I'll just stay with her awhile, I think. We'll redecorate.

She comes close and lowers her voice. "There's Joe," she says. "He's famous."

"Joe who?"

"Joe Fellacio. He sends all the girls to Paris. He's from Hollywood."

"Really!" Over to the left, I see him, a fleshy-faced bald man with a Gorbachev-like red scar on his head. There's a girl with him—I can't see her from behind, just the purple of her paper-thin dress and her short blond hair. She seems young, very young, thin arms, a question mark in the delicate tilt of her head.

"Let's go over there."

She puts a hand over her mouth. "No, he doesn't know us. Who are we?"

"Come on. Let's do a ..." I say, making a sniffing sound. "And then we'll be ready."

Later, I just go over, and put out a hand.

"Godunev!"

He's wrapped a paper napkin around his fat neck; he takes it off, wipes his hands with it, doesn't say a word.

"You're the Mexican Ambassador's assistant," he says at last.

"Me! No, I'm not. Why do you think that?"

"Where have you seen me then? Was it at the Comme des Garcons show at the Olympic Penta? Or in the Tribune?"

"Nowhere. I just came from New York. My girlfriend here ..."

But he doesn't wait for me to finish. "You just got to Russia? Look here," he says, pulling out a newspaper, unfurling it theatrically. "This is my society page. That's me, with Yeltsin's press man, Yastrezhemsky, and there with Gazprom's head Vyachirev.

"What do you think?" he asks, but I'm not paying attention. I'm watching his girl instead; a naif, with large, green eyes, buffed on the edges with purple eyeshadow, she's staring into her cola, blowing air through the straw, bored. She watches the eddies swirl about the drink with a sad fascination, as if her fortune might be gleaned from them. She's beautiful, I think, but so young. Can't be more than sixteen.

"Sit down, sit down, you speak English," he continues. He stares at me for a while, distracted, thinking something. Even before he rubs his hands together and smiles cunningly, I guess what's coming. "How would you like to make some phone calls?" he asks. "We're having a big opening for the Aleksander Blok Casino. Steven Seagal and Chuck Norris will be there, so will Kirkoriev and Alla Pugachova. You just need to call some

American companies like Pepsi, Marlboro, to see if they want to sponsor the event. You know, throw in a few thousand dollars. Tell them all our events are classy, we have the best girls, the top Moscow businessmen. Great way to raise your profile."

I watch his girl get up gingerly, and walk towards the bathroom. Her ass is firm, tight, the line of her panties visible under the dress. I want to run after her and rub her up against the stalls.

"Sure, sure," I tell him. "Anytime, just call me."

Irina's been sitting there quiet, watching us, her hands prim in her lap. Now she pipes up, puts her elbow on the formica table, and says, "Let's buy you a Bailey's. We're celebrating his first day in Russia."

He colors, makes a shucking motion. "No-one buys me rounds. But hey, I'll have a drink."

The Baileys come, but not his girl. Ten minutes later, he can't help frowning, keeps turning in the direction of the toilets. Shakes his head, raises his eyebrows at us; his hands knotted together. Finally, he hands me a bill under the table, and says quickly in my ear, "Give this to Olga. She's having a hard time. I think her ass is a bit sore.

"Go on then," he says, when I just stiffen up. "She might be bleeding, you know."

She's in there, her hair in bangs around her face, neck long and white, standing in front of the mirror with her panties around her knees. She's wiping her face with a balled-up tissue when I enter. She doesn't even attempt to slip her underwear back on when I move next to her. Just stares at my image in the mirror and speaks to it as if it were an old friend. I have that impact sometimes on young girls.

"What will mother say? I don't have another pair, you know."

Here's the $100, I should have said. Buy yourself a pair. But I don't.

"You can borrow mine, you know."

She widens her eyes. Turns towards me. "Really?" She puts a finger to her temple as she thinks for a while. "But what kind do you have? My brother wears those small ones, but some men have something like big shorts there, don't they?" Then, thinking I might not be on her side, adds, "That Joe, he's a bad man, you know!"

"Why?"

"Why? Why?" She thinks about this for a second, shakes her head, and is about to answer with a joke when she bursts into tears. Taking her head in my hands, I massage her scalp, kissing her behind her ears.

"Where are you from?"

"Krasnoyarsk, Siberia. I came down here last week for a beauty contest."

I lean close to him when we're back. How? I ask without asking; just a slight tilt of the head, a grimace of what he'll mistake for respect. At his age, I wonder, how is it done? He senses the question, inclines his head and beams down at me.

"She's fifteen," he announces, as if that were explanation. "I'd like to take her to Paris for her sixteenth birthday."

The girl shuts her eyes.

"You can have her," he announces, feigning insouciance. "I'm done with her." He rolls his eyes. "She's still very tight, don't worry."

Irina turns crimson, narrows her eyes and gapes at the young girl, her gaze lingering at the hard points of the girl's nipples, poking out the chiffon dress.

"That's very generous of you. Thank you. We must be going."

"Call me," he says, handing me a card. "We'll get you working."

I stand up, put an arm around Irina and lead her out of there. How does he make his cash?

Outside it's cold and drab with slush on the ground and the Peking Hotel dark in parts. I sense a room somewhere, a halogen-lit room where dollars are being counted. I'll just fly up there like an angel and flap my wings against the windows.

Irina leans her head against mine. "We haven't spent the money yet.

We still have seven hundred dollars."

"So?"

"So, let's burn it. Let's go to Serebryanny Vek."

Irina wants to give everything she's got to possess the long-stemmed rose, which is auctioned off every night to the highest bidder at this joint. She's made up her mind, and she's fucked up. She walks straight into the toilets when we arrive, emerging with so much lipstick that I don't want to kiss her. "Kiss me, kiss me, Godunev," she cries, and presses her face against mine, leaving reddish streaks everywhere. Then she fights with the waiter for the divan nearest the stage. "He just came from New York," she says, and struggles to pull my passport out of my jacket pocket until I silence her with a quick pinch on her buttocks.

They're all losers here. Small-time gangsters with peroxide blondes from the end of the metro line. Their dates bang their flossed lips together and gape at their men, grateful. They don't like Irina. I can tell that. She's set herself up against them, staring proudly ahead, ruffling her hair, seductive. Readying herself to outbid them, to humiliate them with her largesse. Irina, I say, stroking her hand but she brushes it away. She's untouchable right now, convinced that this is her debut. You're a provincial girl, I think, still excited that you're a player in the supposed world of the big city.

But everyone's like her, I notice. They're all eager, itching to pull something out their pockets, measuring each other as though this were the Olympics. Bilyaet. There's only one who's not like them, cashmere sweater and Armani jacket, sitting next to a mousy man in shades and a Vyssotsky leather jacket who stares straight ahead, chomping on sunflower seeds. The pony-tailed Armani man, dark-skinned, maybe Georgian, has this pose of ennui, of the sophisticate. But I think he's not relaxed, he's just trying hard to look like a Parisian—there are little worry lines on his forehead and grey in his sideburns. When I look over at him, give a knowing wink, he looks away. So I wave now, make funny shapes with my hand, project their shadows against the wall.

I'm high as it is. How come they're not having fun?

When the sequined lady comes on stage with the long rose, it's a let-down. Irina squints at it, tries to discern something special in its shape, hue or brightness. But there's nothing, it's just a rose, a Russian rose, with slightly wilted petals. There's a collective sigh, an exhalation of disappointment—and then the bidding starts. It's lackluster at first, no-one wants to pay for that rose. It all seems so ridiculous, I can tell.

But then a flushed, big-jowled man stands up and waves a hundred dollar bill in the air, and they crane to look. One hundred and thirty, shouts someone else, and it begins in earnest. The money itself is the aphrodisiac now. With all these numbers being thrown about, the rose transforms, glowing in the light from above as if it were stuffed with rubies. Even I feel it's become so much more delightful and valuable in the past minutes that I'm now desperate to put it in my lapel and walk out of here. Stroke its thin, avocado-green stem and prick my fingers against its thorns. Ah, life.

I'm so lost in these thoughts that I don't realize the bidding's gone up to five hundred, and there's just Irina and the Armani man. He's quite humorless, raising the ante fifty dollars each time. Five hundred and fifty. Six hundred. I realize Irina's got to stop soon, and so I semaphore over to him. Stop it, I plead with my eyes, this means something to the girl. She's from Saratov, she wants to feel she's part of the sound of the big city. Nada.

So I just—and this is spur of the moment—slip a hand past the armholes of Irina's sleeveless black dress. Fishing it over the collarbone, I grab her left breast and pop it out quick, flashing it at the Armani man. It's all so fast she doesn't even notice, she's pushed forwards, face flushed, watching him and the rose as if her life depended on it. But he does; and he smiles for the first time, as if we had just concluded a business deal. I can tell he likes that, or at least he wants to pretend he can appreciate such gestures. He goes all happy, and does a little dance with his shoulders at me. Then standing up theatrically, he drops his napkin against the ground.

Six hundred and fifty dollars.

Irina's so thrilled she lopes up to the stage quickly and does a victory thing, pumping her hand out in the air. "Please, can you stand still for a moment," asks the woman, so Irina drops her hands to her side and turns to face us, so jittery that she trembles slightly as the other threads the stem through her hair. When she's done, my girl's so moved she wants to give a speech. "Dear Muscovites, hello from Saratov. They make the best toy airplanes there, as you know. I just want to say I grew up with roses, our dacha had a rose garden, and it's true girls like "roses and shrimps" best. But this one is the best, the most special; it's also my first Moscow rose."

Post-speech, she turns melancholic. Hanging her head, she strides back to our table and buries her face in my lap. How could I not love her then? I have these images in my head—not Goya or Degas this time—but of the late, cynical Repin and the Volga Bargemen. Hard, unforgiving light, muscles of the damned men straining, their faces contorted. Irina's nothing like that, but the intensity of her emotions is the same—and it touches me. I want violence, just a sliver of it, a gasp of pain. I get like this when I'm moved, want to push the feeling to its limits. So I bunch the skin of her delicate neck together and twist it until she pushes her head against my legs. "Hurt me," she jests. "Hurt me more."

Outside she walks so proud, the rose held in front of her like a Russian icon. Khrestny Chod. I picture us walking barefoot through the spring slush of some peasant village in the steppes, curs yapping, and a woman frying mushrooms in a big pot. Hundreds of others behind us, straining to catch a glimpse of the six-hundred-and-fifty-dollar rose, the sacrificial lamb. "I'm so happy," she says, unbuttoning her jacket to the cold. "When we were little, we used my visit my uncle Vasya in the country. He was a drunk, such a mad drunk, oi, the whole day he just cackled and abused us, sending mother into tears. I used to sit on the window sill outside his bedroom with his cat in my lap, this kind of small, black, kitten, one eye damaged, spots of gray on it ..."

"Wait," I say, pulling her closer. "What's happening over there?"

"What? Where?"

"There." I gesture at the crowd gathering down the end of the street. Police cars are approaching, it seems, the sound of their sirens rending the air. "Oh my God, what could it be?" she cries. Linking hands, we break into a half-trot, half-run, pushing through the others at the edge. Glass shards on the street, beneath the front right window of a black smashed Mercedes 600. Robbery, I think, before I catch sight of the blood, a just-visible scar running down the black door of the car. There's more on the pavement, congealed into a bleached Japanese flag. I move closer, lean forwards, thinking "Serves the mafia right." But it's him, the Armani-clad altruist from the club, his head against the neck of the leather seat, and his blood-drenched ponytail still dripping. He's been shot in the stomach too, the sweater torn open in parts; the seatbelt's still holding though, keeping him rigid. His face is calm, simple in death, uncomplicated. His death marks him as just another striver, an opportunist, for whom things spun out of control.

"Contract killing," someone mutters.

As I move back, Irina presses close, crossing herself. "So young, so good," she says, a few feet from the car, and wipes her eyes. "Let's go," I suggest. "Wait, wait, I'm thinking." An idea striking her, she walks quickly to the car, places the rose against his chest and comes running back. "It's so much better with him," she says crying. "He was so good, so young."

I notice the mousy man watching us from the driver's side, so we cross over and walk to him. He's still chewing sunflower seeds. "Sorry," I say. "He was super, a great man. What little we know."

He twiddles with his mustache. "Nothing. It's not your problem. These things happen."

Irina seems the only one distraught. She tugs at me, puts a finger to my head. "It's his first day in Russia and he must see this. This is the land of miracles."

He shrugs again, sweet-natured. "Go," he says, forceful though, when the police cars come swerving around the corner. "Go soon or you're in trouble."

When we turn the corner, Irina wraps herself against the side of a building, and bawls. "I don't want Russia," she screams. "I want to leave. I want a normal country. I don't want to be part of this madness. I WANT TO LE.. LEAVE. You something understand, do you Godunev?"

Holding her by the waist, I kiss her ears. I haven't felt so fine in years, not since I first arrived in America, and traded anecdotes with a Russian cab driver at JFK. It's unfair that she can't see that, that like all the rest here she imagines that it's just klassna over there. If only they knew.

"You don't understand, do you?" I whisper. "The West isn't the paradise all you Russians think. It's like the Brezhnev era there, stagnant, stultified. Like ancient Athens. Nothing happens in America, believe me, except for television. Everything that is to be done has been done, so everyone's frustrated. All they do is obsess about their past, divvy it up into decades, and get endlessly nostalgic about it. It smells of shit there. Here," I say, widening my arms, "it's the third Rome. It's all a new beginning, there's space for someone like me. You understand, don't you?"

"Understand? Understand what?" She murmurs, quietly stiffening in my arms.

"Hear me?" I ask. A police car swerves round a corner in the distance, its siren fading mournfully as it moves away. She opens her eyes, squints at me, wipes tears off her cheeks with the back of her hand. Without warning she giggles, or tries to giggle. I can't be sure.

"Understand what?" she asks harsh. "That you're a selfish Russian bastard? Don't fool me, Godunev. I'm not so stupid as you think. You're just an asshole like the rest of them." She balls her hand into a fist and pummels me on the shoulder, then starts in on my face, clawing my cheeks with her nails.

"Just an asshole," she repeats, and scratches me harder, falling against me as she does so.

"Enough, enough. Stop acting like some valuta whore," I shout, but she goes ahead anyway, biting a finger so hard I gasp out. "Stop, please," I plead, and she releases it. Grins victorious. Her greenish eyes are Aphrodite's, inscrutable, arrogant. She pokes me in the ribs, pulls at the Prada jacket.

"You were a loser before, Godunev. Think you're like Boris Godunov hah! You diss the West now, but what were you before? Just some kiosk romantic, stupid, no idea of how the world worked. Why you think I left you for that American? Because you were a bore, a stupid patriot like all the rest." She sneers, holds her head high. "And now you've got a little bit of style. Even those biznismen were impressed yesterday. So why did you come back? You got chased out, hah? Got involved in the wrong deal, kicked out of America?"

"Fuck you. You're just a whore. Don't dare talk to me like that." I turn and strut away, hands in my pockets, whistling an old song out of tune. She's just a cunt, let her go her own way. I'll do something, I'll show them all that I'm not just a loser, that I can be part of what's happening here. There's a building ahead, late 19th century, Doric columns framing its entrance portico. A plaque to the left of the iron door reads "Institute of Horticulture, Study of Rare Flowers." I run a hand along its embossed brass, pause at the Russian I's and caress them. My mother was a naturalist, a hippie who pointed out all the flowers when I was a kid. "That's lilac," she used to say. "Find a five-petaled flower and you can make a wish." I'm trying to conjure up an irregular purple petal, when someone grabs me from behind.

"You fool," she cries, laughing, burying her face in my shoulders. "I'm your only chance to do something here. Don't you understand that?

We'd make a great team. The two of us, we'd rock the town."

I eye her, wary, struck again by her sexiness, by her horny vibe. Fuck you, I want to cry out, but instead, I edge forward and bite her lips. She bites back, grabbing my erection, unzipping my velvet pants and stroking. "We'll make a team," she repeats, kissing my forehead. "Just don't betray me ever, you understand that. Don't you?"

The phone rings, its harsh Grande Valse tune breaking our intimacy. She rustles inside her Louis Vuitton handbag, pulls it out, brings it to her ears. "Hallyo."

She motions a ssshhh with her index finger, whispers, "Yuri Salminsky," and walks a few paces away. When she returns, she's radiant, jovial even. "What he want?"

"He's lonely, he wants company."

"Payecchali k nim. Let's go then."

minus twenty one

When we walk in there, still drunk and high, adrenaline-rushed from the murder, a yob in a checked shirt turns to us quick and then looks away, as if he were sorry about something. A hush descends on the flashy apartment with its leopard-skin couches in the living room, cupid-patterned curtains and billiard table with golden legs. One of two girls, most likely sisters, both wearing electric-blue plastic T-shirts, sticks her tongue out at me. Irina tightens her grip on my shoulder when Yuri Salminsky comes out of a side-room, shirtless, a heavy chain around his neck.

Without speaking, his finger over his lips, he pulls me aside and drags me into the kitchen. Tiptoes, so his face is level with mine, widens his eyes and taps the side of his head with his thumb.

"They'll kill you," he says, very soft. "They'll cut you into small pieces and feed you to the dogs. They'll tie you to a horse and quarter you," he adds, his voice rising.

He steps forward, tugs at the collar of my jacket. "Pashol nachyui, durak, jibatse," he swears. "They saw you, hanging around the car, planting that rose. They even photographed you," he says, croaking like a war veteran. He waves his finger in the air. "They don't like this. They don't like this at all.

"What are you going to do about it?"

Shrugging, I turn up the collar of my jacket.

"Who saw me? If they were really professionals, they'd have seen we were just messing around. Nothing serious."

He taps his finger on my forehead. "Don't act smart with me. I don't have time for big talkers."

I leer at him until he's ready to strike and then clap my hands casual. "We're here as guests aren't we? Do you have some pernod here?"

"Pernod? What is that? What are you talking about? You listen to me," he screams, tugging at my lapels, "they'll send you to the emergency ward if you act like this."

But I just stare at him, placid, smile with my eyes. They're gray. "Pernod is a substitute for absinthe. Its special taste comes from badiane and fennel oils; the French drink it with water." Then I slouch over to the table where there're some bottles stacked and poke around. I learned back in the kiosk days, when the Chechens came around on Fridays for handouts, that it doesn't do to show fear, especially when you're cornered. That just makes them bolder, stokes their anger.

"Ah, you do have some," I exclaim, and begin unscrewing the cap. He comes over, hovers around, sniffs at me as he leans his weight against the table. My nonchalance confuses him.

"Want some?" I pour some into a glass and run a finger through it. Lick the wet forefinger. "Ah! I could be back in the Montmartre."

"You know," I say, tapping a foot against the floor, "my father loved cards. He really loved cards. Even gambled, way back when, in the Soviet times, while I sat on his lap. Didn't want to go home, just sat there for hours, hiding in his big sable coat."

Widening his eyes, he stops, stares and then goes aah. I can almost see him beginning to understand what I want him to realize—that I come from a mob family. He doesn't quite believe it at first, watches me some more while I sip at the pernod, tapping out a tune with my feet.

"So," he says at last, "you've got protection. No wonder you're as cool as a vor v zakone." He spreads his arm outwards. "Tell me something—only the truth. Did you really arrive from New York yesterday?"

"I'm from New York. I got me a five dollar on the Yankees," I rap out. "Pernod! You want some? It's good."

He comes up to me and puts his face close to mine again, so close I can see the yellowish asterisks near the floor of his eyes; they're like ships adrift in a white sea.

"This doesn't leave the room. None of what has been said." Then he relaxes, moves back, glides his head from side to side like a dancer in the Hindi films. "Godunev, good to make your acquaintance. I'm just a bankir, not a killyer at all. Sometimes you just have to know who people are. We live in such times. What can I do about it? But tell me something," he says, rubbing his hands together. "The rose was quite funny. Whose idea was that? Yours or Irina's?"

"Irina's."

He closes his eyes and brings his arms outwards slowly. "I knew it. She's not a simple girl, not at all. There's something of Dr. Zhivago's Lara about her."

"You think! Nastasya Fillipovna, perhaps."

"Then, who is Prince Myshkin? You?" He rubs his hands together and cackles; sighs. "Oi, the classics, who cares about them these days. Godunev, fate must have sent you to us."

"Who killed him?"

He narrows his eyes. "Irina's our friend. We've known her for a while." He winks. "We know most of the working girls!

"How about you? Are you going to be our friend?"

When I nod assent, he massages me on the shoulder. "Let's drink to our friendship then."

We down three shots of vodka without pause. "Ah, that was good," he says, his eyes steamed up. "That was very good. You can also drink, even after America. Give me your hand." He pushes his hand with its elbow crooked under mine so that they're locked together in an embrace. "Let's drink again now. Brudershaft. Solntsevo mafia," he says quickly when we're done. "He was trying to break into the oil trading—and other, which I can't talk about—businesses. He might have succeeded had he given them some gifts. But he was too busy spending his cash on other things, buying roses for example. So vot," he says, mock-slashing his throat with his finger.

"Tell me something, what were you doing there today?"

I clap him on the shoulder, whisper something he can't hear to confuse him, and then jerk back, rock a bit on the balls of my feet. "Blowing your thousand dollars as fast as we could," I say at last.

Then I just turn on my heels and walk out the kitchen, banging the door behind me. He thought I was a dunce, did he! Is that what they all think? Just because I don't wear double-breasted suits and crimson-tinted eyeglasses. I stop at the billiard table, pick up a ball, and clutch it in my left hand as I walk towards Irina.

"He was so young, so good," she's saying in English to the yob as I approach. He's dressed the hick in a loose flannel shirt untucked, a dirty white T-shirt sticking out from underneath. His hair's like straw, flopped over his head; his teeth are rust-colored near the gums. He's trying hard to capture that Seattle grunge look.

"Hi!"

"Arkady."

"Godunev."

"You're a Nirvana fan?" I blurt. I guess he senses the undertone of anger in the question because he ignores me, just keeps on chatting with Irina. When I ask the question again, louder, he turns to me, spits with a vengeance into a plastic cup at his side, and then puts a restraining hand on my knee.

"We're just chatting about what happened. I'm cool. You're cool too?"

"He's the son of that famous dissident writer," whispers Irina into my ear.

"Which one?"

When she mentions the name, I exhale slowly, sit back, and give him a second look. "So you got bored of America?"

"That was a long time ago. How about you? Irina said you just arrived," he says, appraising me as if I were a foreigner. The skin over his high cheekbones is rough and crimson, like a bruise. There's still something Yankish about him as he assesses me, very self-consciously trying to figure me out. He rests his eyes on the sisters for a second before continuing.

"Wanted to get in on the action here? This place is booming right now, just like in Moore's law. There's twice as many bars and restaurants every six months. You came at the right time. I remember when the kiosks were the only places to buy alcohol at all. Or when we'd fly to Helsinki to do our grocery shopping."

He takes a clump of black tobacco from a pouch and packs it under his lower lip. I can't tell whether his demeanor is genuine or some Moscow affectation. That bothers me.

"I came back because I jumped bail," I tell him.

He studies me intently for a moment—his eyes in rare focus—and then leans back. "Lots of people here for those reasons. You met that pervert, Fellacio? He's wanted by the FBI, I hear, for rape and mail fraud. Can't ever go back to the States. There's no extradition treaty with the United States, so you'll never have a problem."

The twin sisters are on the neighboring couch in identical papier-mâché skirts and plastic T-shirts. One's prettier than the other, with limpid eyes, fuller lips. The other's thinner, more eager and girlish.

"What do you want to do here?"

"I want to stand on the St. Petersburg highway and sell watermelons."

He spits again into the paper cup at his side. "You better think about a different get-up. You'd be robbed blind your first day." Even Irina giggles at this crack; doesn't even apologize with her eyes when I turn to reprimand her.

So I stand up, walk over to the twins, and shove the pool ball into the less cute one's skirt. She chortles, winks at me, then pulls the ball from under the skirt and rolls it between her sister's thighs. The other just sits still for a while, savors the feeling of that cold enameled surface, brings her legs together. Then she extracts it and throws it quick at me. I catch it, and lob it at the famous writer's son. He's stunned, impotently watches the ball fly towards him, jerks away when it comes close. It hits him on the shoulder and rolls down his crumpled shirt, settling between the legs of his jeans. Irina picks it up and licks it, salaciously. He just stares at her, speechless.

"You Americans, a bit squeamish aren't you?" I say in Russian. Then I go over to the stereo and put on Nevermind, just to rile him up. He takes the ball from Irina, holds it gingerly in his palm, and walks to the pool table.

"Game?" he asks.

"Nah! I make up my own games," I say. I stride past him and onto the balcony. It's freezing outside, but beyond the upward incline of the roof, hemmed in by a low railing, is the Kremlin and its crenellated brick walls. It's the back view of the Kremlin, I can't see the smaller gate fronting Aleksandrovy Sad, where the Bolsheviks had gunned their way into the edifice. Down on the street below, the passing cars make trails of light as they plow through the slushy road. I can see the embankment on the Yauza canal; and far down, I can just make out the arched bridge, shaped like a horse-shoe, where I went after work back in the kiosk days, to smoke a joint and watch the water eddy in the spring breeze.

"I used to live here," he says, coming up besides me. "Downstairs. It was the artists' building in Soviet times. We used to joke, though, that it was a holding cell; most of my neighbors were sent to prison." He chuckles. "We were luckier. Just given a one-way ticket out of here. I remember we left a small Dalmatian behind with the guard of the building. Wonder what happened to it?"

"You like dogs?"

He nods. "I hate them," I say, and turn back to the apartment. When I'm inside I go straight to the twins, and pulling them off the couch, hoist them onto the billiard table. Then I go to the stereo and turn the radio dial to 106.8, pumping an arm forward to the techno beat.

"Godunev," Irina asks, pulling me down besides her. "What's going on? Why so aggressive?" She's concerned, I can tell; her nose twitches when she's a bit stressed, I've begun to notice. "It'll be all right. Everything is klassna."

Then I stumble to the table and start voguing with the two girls. They're just going through the motions at first, their arms flailing in the air, but when Salminsky comes into the room, still shirtless, and the song changes to a Snap number, they pick up speed.

"Davai, davai, davai," he goes, and they jump around, twirl in the air, embrace each other, bring their lips together for an instant, and then separate with a shove, cartwheeling backwards on the narrow top. I go up to one and try to pull her top off, her sister follows my cue and does the same, helping me pull her twin's T-shirt off. Boom, it's done, and she's in her bra, whirling around. Then it's the other one's turn, and this time Irina comes to help, holding her butt, stroking it, while I lift up the plastic top.

When they're both topless, Irina gets friskier, jumping up on the table with them, and throwing her arms forward as if she were playing volleyball.

"How did you start all this?" asks Salminsky, visibly excited. "You're a genius." Taking some bills out of his pocket, he throws Benjamins at the girls like an Eastern potentate. The twins bend down and grab them, stuff them down their skirts. Irina just watches the bills come floating down, but keeps up her dancing, stamping them with her heels when she can.

"For you, for you," goes Salminsky, and walking over, hands her a hundred. She waves her hand, dances some more, seductive, then bends down, takes the bill from him and flashes it before her eyes like Uma Thurman in Pulp Fiction. He claps, as does Arkady who's just come in from the balcony. Irina just winks at Yuri, smiles meaningfully at me, and takes the note, crumples it up, and pops it into her mouth. She jumps off the table then, goes up to me, and starts kissing me wild, feeding me bits of green paper. They're rough against the roof of the mouth, but as we chew upon them, they turn soggy, soft, go easy down the gullet. When we're done, we stand arm in arm and stick our tongues out at the gathering.

Davai. Davai. Davai.

On the way back, we're so high we could snap into two and it wouldn't matter. We'd just multiply again like earthworms. We sit close in the cab, not speaking, our arms around each other. She seems older now, Irina, more relaxed, shorn of that girlish nervousness. Her eyelids are like steamed pelmenis to me, warm and tan. I kiss them lightly, so that they flutter restlessly.

There was an orgy. In the jacuzzi upstairs, all six of us, crammed in there, the twins with their tongues entwined, putting on a show. "I'm older, I'm older by 20 minutes and so Lara will do whatever I want," said the older one, instructing her sister to pleasure Irina, her hand around the engorged dick of the writer's son. He was the worst, blabbing the whole time. Kazakhstan and the Baltics. The Russians still stuck there, robbed of their nationhood by the collapsing Soviet Union. Yeltsin should have annexed those parts of the empire for Russia, claimed them early before things settled down.

Shut up. Shut up. But he wouldn't. It was the coke, I was sure, it made him voluble. So we hid it from him, just fed him vodka and champagne instead, until he slowed down, settled against the edge of the tub, tongue sticking out like a dog's. That's when Salminsky had turned to me, fluffed my hair.

"Godunev, Godunev, you can talk. I can't deny that. Noh, I have a proposal for you. A big proposal. Are you ready?"

A party, I think now, as the taxi speeds down Bolshaya Polyanka. A huge bash with the St. Petersburg rock band Aukstsion and strippers and DJs from London. A hundred grand to spend. I like that very much. I shake Irina, wake her up from her slumber.

"It's going to be the best tusovka Moscow's ever seen."

Nodding sleepily, she kisses me on the lips. "You've been lucky." She shakes her head. "I'm also so lucky we met. Prosto tak. Like something falling from the skies."

Menya povezlo. I got lucky, I think. Are you sure? asks a small voice somewhere. Who are these people? Can you trust them? You'll get caught up in their affairs, drawn into their sordid lives. Soon you'll be so involved, so trussed up, that you won't be able to escape. You'll spend your cash on roses to feel free and then you'll be shot also, right through the head, empty as a used vial of crack.

Instead I gaze out through the frosted window at the passing city. Near Dobrininskaya, I think we've taken a wrong turn and ended up on the Arbat. There are neon signs flashing near the Orthodox Church; a gold-and-pink monstrosity, Christmas light framing its windows, juts out onto the street. A Snickers ad looms above us as we cross the ring road. There's a new McDonald's, a line still snaking around it at this time of night. A man stands on the corner, almost in the street; it's so bright in the night, I can read the Chicago Bulls lettering on his sweatshirt under the leather jacket. When we pass I see he's holding up a Russian Playboy, a lone magazine wrapped in plastic, waving it at the passing cars.

Moscow's changed. Even the snow-crusted kiosks and copper stars over the metro are different than they were. It's a mood shift in the city I struggle to capture when it hits me like a bulb going off: it's the light, that's what changed! It's so fucking light—this city is now bathed in it, frolicking in all this luminous energy. All that oil and gas pumped here from Siberia and Nenets and the far reaches of the Barents Sea converted into electricity, and then shot through wires and tungsten filaments until it kills the night. The Kremlin's lit up like a strip bar, the ring roads are all alight, and there are billboards shining down on the street like reflectors for a fashion shoot. It's bizarre, this light, so unnatural here, like the background glow of a Renaissance painting. That's what it is, this radiance, some sort of lighthouse beacon. Beckoning us all to our dreams, our secret aspirations.

I lean forwards and tap the cabby on the shoulder.

"So much light in Moscow. It's become like Las Vegas."

"And so," he answers gruff, meeting my eye in the rearview mirror. "So what. The miners in Kamchatka haven't been paid their wages in months, all those factories in the Urals are shut down, their workers not even having enough bread for a living. Everywhere in our gigantic nation people are drinking themselves to death because there's nothing else to do. Chechens are exploding bombs in the metro, wanting to humiliate us, turn us into a third-world outhouse. Our best Russian girls are spreading their legs for Georgians and black asses on the streets here. And Moscow is sucking all the blood of Russia to itself, like a vampire, to feed its greed. Mayor Yuri Luzhkov, he's a bandit, grabbing everything from the regions. Soon they'll take so much that our Russian heart will stop beating, it'll just collapse. And you think it's good that there's light on the street?"

"Are you some kind of foreigner?" he mumbles to himself.

When we get back to her apartment, I stagger in, run my hands down its floral-patterned wallpaper.

"This place sucks."

"Yeah, right," she says, coming up behind me, nipping my ear. "You think I'm trailer trash, don't you? Just a hillbilly chick from the provinces, trying to make it in the big city.

"And you're what, Mr. Godunev. Kiosk trash. That's what you were, and that's what you are now. Don't forget that. Don't go about putting on airs around me. You'd be back there if it weren't for tonight. Now you can become a promoter, a party organizer. Isn't that what you always wanted?"

I whirl around, consider hitting her, but then decide against it when a trenchant line comes to mind instead. "And what are you? Whore trash? Life isn't like Pretty Woman, I'm not your Richard Gere. Nothing's gonna change just because I've entered your life. It'll be the same all over again." Triumphant, I turn to the windows of her balcony, whistle the tune to "Stand By Me."

We're behaving just like Yanks, gotta shed that side of me. I primp my shoulders, tense my neck muscles to appear tougher, when she appears behind me, pushes me onto the carpet, and pummels me on the chest and stomach, sobbing all the time. "You bastard, you fucker, bilyaet, everything's a joke to you isn't it?" Her face is contorted, snapped out of shape; I'm so fucked from the jetlag and everything else, I just lie there, drooling spit from my mouth, weakly fighting off her blows. Her nails pinch the space between my left ribs and I moan, attempt to defend myself, when she stops without warning. She turns soft, her sobs become more protracted, and she's supine over me, stroking my chest hairs.

"It's so good being with you, Godunev. You wouldn't understand how lonely it can be here. We're both aliens, corrupted, not like them at all. You'll understand that after a while."

I just go all numb, tears spring out my eyes. I grab her around the buttocks and squeeze them sensually. It has been a while since there was intimacy, feels so good, so good. I remember the hard, mad stare I had in those days. New York, Miami, Tel Aviv. The jobs selling nutmeg, thieving gasoline to hawk on the street corners of Brighton Beach. The long empty nights; the occasional Puerto Rican girl who couldn't even speak English. Loco Russo, they said. El Loco Russo. Sometimes I'd head to the downtown New York clubs like Spy Bar and Pravda, and fob off these glamorous alter egos on the gullible models from the American Mid West. Convince them I was a masochistic German pornographer, or a Finnish race car driver. Come mornings though, I'd be too knackered to keep up the pretense, and would beat a hasty retreat to Brooklyn, to its dive bars and its fast-talking hustlers from Odessa.

We're on the bed before I know it, going at each other. "You can dominate me if you like," she keeps saying. "Just tell me what you want me to do from now on. And I'll do it. I'll be a good Russian girl. I'll make pelmeni and borscht, and I won't ever go out. I'll just sit here and watch television and polish my nails."

"Ira, Ira," I choke out. "I love you."

Standing outside her varnished metal door in the Trump Tower, a Hechler and Koch pistol in a black Gucci handbag slung around my neck, I think back to that night. Our first real night together, when the possibility that our lives might become entwined hung suspended in the air like the smoke from our Parliament Lights. We lay there until dawn, limbs tangled, and joked about Gena the cartoon crocodile; got high, and kissed, her tongue pushing mine aside, going further, further, until all thought was shut out. She should have told me then that she was in deep, deeper than I imagined. But she didn't.

The little bitch. She just waltzed through life, her desires leading the way. At first, she wanted me around because she could use me, so stupid of me not to see that. I wasn't as tough as the Russians, an Americanized hippie from the past, still a bit of a romantic. With my old school Pink Floyd and Uriah Heep tastes, my stoner idealism from perestroika days still alive, I was an anachronism in mid-90s Moscow. She was stronger, or so she thought, she could bend me to her will. And it tickled her that I made her laugh. It was like that with all the rest. They liked me around because I put them at ease, unselfconscious as I was. And not as New Russian-ified as the rest of them, because I hadn't been around those years.

I didn't realize how terrified they all were at the time of appearing foolish, of failing in their New Russian roles. I caught a glimpse of that with Yuri Salminsky sometimes. His fear, for instance, when I suggested just stopping his Merc and getting pissed at a kiosk somewhere; an almost visceral terror that someone might notice him. So we'd drive out somewhere far, Tver—a hundred miles from Moscow—and act like country bumpkins, getting trashed on cheap Rasputin vodka and rolling around in the snow. "I love you, I love you, Godunev," he'd say, and sing a horrible Tom Waits tune, "Waltzing Mathilda" perhaps, off-key and cheesy. That's when I think he was happiest: not slapping his arm around someone's shoulder at a glitzy bash with topless models pouring Hennesey Cognac but rolling around in the snow.

But all that's now so far away. At the time I just wanted a lightness of being after the dead seriousness of America. What I didn't know is that when life is so light there's nothing to stop it from coming crashing down. And in Russia, nothing happens by accident either—every little pleasure extracts its fee.

She sensed that at the very beginning. "Don't change, Godunev," she begged that night, licking my temple with her granulated tongue. "Don't become like them. They'll want you to but stay the way you are. It's better that way." But then she did everything she could to bring me inside a circle where corruption was one of the passwords. Closer and closer I came to the center, until I was deserted, left alone, so others wouldn't take the blame. She just wanted to leave, secure her future.

So I'll kill her, I reason, running my pinkie along the numbers embossed on her faux-wood steel door. That's how I'll avenge the past.

minus eighteen

If I were to describe Kirk's apartment again I'd be even more of a bastard. But nothing's changed otherwise. It's still the same as I pictured it during that first Aeroflot flight out of Russia: the whiter-than-white walls; the Ikea couch with its once-hip striped linen covering; and the hardwood floors so clean—I remember I had wanted to squat down and lick them.

But details aside, everything's different. This time around the décor doesn't turn me envious as it once did, or rebuke me with its evocation of a superior America. Neither does it inspire me to spout eloquent on Dostoevsky and Tolstoy, or defend Russian culture. That's it, I think. This is all it was. Just some small bourgeois cool apartment. Nothing else. Not even something special—a jacuzzi or a billiard table; some designer chairs. That's it? No, can't be. I take a deep breath and cast around for something of that past envy. Not there. Not in the couch or the walls at least. Ah, there! I discover a whiff of that "fucking-rich Yankee!" feeling in the large CD collection stacked high near the stereo.

But it passes. And I'm left numb again, thinking idly that the silver chain I just bought, the one with an Om pendant, is kruta.

"So," I say at last, "you're still living here."

He sort of laughs into his cupped hands. Hasn't changed much either: the same flannel shirt and blue jeans worn loose around the ass. Still a bit shy, averting his glance in mid-sentence.

"I got a good deal. Expats coming these days are paying twice as much for the same apartment." I think he'll stop at this point but he seems keen to convince me further. "This is a great neighborhood. You're right in the center and the metro is just a ten-minute walk away. I love going to Krisis Zhanra on Mondays when all the provincials aren't there." He points at the CD collection and his books against the wall. "I've got all this stuff here. Such a hassle moving." He averts his gaze again, glares at the balcony and then shrugs. "Sun comes in the morning when I'm waking up. Can't complain."

"Yeah." I sit down without asking him and cross my legs, wanting him to see that I'm wearing silk Valentino socks. I'm not sure he notices. I'm feeling good, very comfortable. Condescension is cool—it brings out the comedian in me. I play with my shades a bit, slide them back over my eyes, and groove around as if I'm in a nightclub. Then I chuckle. "What difference does it make? Home is where the ass is warm. That's what we Russians say. It's warm here, isn't it?"

"That's the best thing about this place. The heating's just right, not too hot like in some apartments."

Having come to ask him what happened with Irina, I'm beginning to understand. It seems obvious she couldn't have stayed with this loser for long. Yanks, I think, you've had your heyday. I know there was a time when all the Russian girls were throwing themselves at you and you were the White Gods, but it's over, isn't it?

But I just say. "I read your article in the Moscow Times about the chess-crazed governor of Kalmykia. When I was drunk one night I thought, let's go. I had some crazy plan of gifting Ilumzhinov a pair of Alan Mikli shades."

He giggles to deflect the implied compliment. "That was a wild trip." Throws his head back in reflection, and smiles confidently at me. "I'm writing features these days—much more interesting than plain reporting. If I were in the States, I couldn't be doing this stuff."

Putting the shades back on, I stare at him, thinking that it's about time he should notice the Om pendant. It seems to unnerve him, though—my passivity, that is—so he just smokes, shooting covert glances at me. After a while, he leans forward and blows smoke into my face.

"It was crazy there. There was a big party with beautiful Kalmyk whores for everyone. We took them into the sauna and fucked them. The provinces, that's where it's happening. Moscow girls are getting too difficult."

"You fuck whores? What kind of American are you? You're not a feminist?"

"Of course I fuck whores. Everyone does in Moscow. It's the best part about living here."

"Me not. I'm a whore myself." Putting an arm around his shoulder, I pull him closer. "Let's not talk about shit. Let's drink some vodka instead. To our meeting again. I haven't changed so much."

So we start to drink. Stolichnaya vodka. In the beginning I think I'll leave after a couple shots; crack a joke about his relationship with Irina, and then walk out of there with my head held high. But after a hundred grams of vodka or so I realize I'm enjoying myself. Until he puts on some King Crimson, Three of a Perfect Pair. It was my favorite album once, he knows that, but now its moody anachronistic melancholia jars, bringing back the times when I was a silly romantic. "Turn it off, turn it off," I shout, blocking my ears. "It's so dated.

Don't you have any Kruger & Dorfmeister albums, some DJ Crush, the new acid jazz stuff?"

His face takes on a strange expression. "That's what all those New Russians are into, all that techno stuff. I never quite got into it."

"Yeah, so what, it's more cutting-edge than all that late-60s crap, which was cool only when it was banned."

He comes closer, runs a finger across the sleeve of my Prada jacket. Whistles low.

"You've gotten pretty New Russian yourself. What's happened?"

"What do you think?" I snap. "Where have you been living? This is a different planet than it was four or even three years ago. We've just gotten too smart to act like Yanks any more, to look up to America, go to cheesy sports' bars. Get with the flow, or you'll be left out."

Sucking in his cheeks, he gets up, and snaps his fingers distracted. "Maybe you're right." His voice falters. "I'm just not quite so trendy as all the rest, can't reinvent myself just like that. I'm a journalist after all—got some ideals." He goes to the stereo, puts on some David Bowie and fidgets, waiting for me to speak.

"You're all merchants of doom, all you Western journalists, writing about the disaster stories, peddling our misfortunes to the West. Lighten up, smell the roses here sometimes."

He listens to me intently, then gets up and paces the room. "There's a guy called Mark Ames here," he says, who started this rag—the eXile—it's all about clubs, sex with young Russian girls, taking amphetamines. Thinks he's Hunter Thompson, hanging around cool clubs like Ptyuch. I think about that sometimes, getting closer to the scene. There's a lot of stuff happening, isn't there?"

Strange. I want to bend down and kiss him on the forehead and tell him I love him. Americans can be losers, but there's one good thing about them: you can expose yourself a bit, act goofy, show them how your mind works, and they'll think it's cool. And then you can be sure they'll forget everything you told them by the next morning. With Russians it's different: you might just get a bullet in the head.

"So what happened with Irina?" I want to ask. But instead I saunter over to his desk where there's a framed picture of them standing besides a seated Ronald McDonald. Kirk's holding up a Big Mac in one hand, his other arm around her thin waist, bare in a Mickey Mouse tank top. Hands limp at her sides, she's gazing to the left of the picture; checking out her reflection in a mirror, I'm sure. She seems radiant though, glowing from the inside, and amused at this fast food photo shoot. Her head is inclined towards him so that strands of her silken hazel hair brush against his baseball cap. Happier times!

"She's beautiful, isn't she? When I was back in America for a while I forgot how gorgeous Russian girls can be." He makes a little clicking sound in his throat, and shifts on the couch. "We were the one millionth customers to the Pushkin McDonalds. Can you imagine that? It's the biggest outlet in the world after the one in Shanghai. They gave us a month's worth of Big Mac meals in honor of the occasion. Eeee yaa, imagine that. You're a winner, boy," he drawls, putting on a Texan accent. He's trying to remain ironic, keep his emotional distance. Get me to start tittering with him and drop the probing. But I don't smile as I would in America. I'm a New Russian now and I don't need to please Yanks. I just pick up the picture and shake it in his face.

"And?" I stand before him and gesture. "What happened?"

"What do you mean, man? What was supposed to happen?"

"About Irina? Where did she go?"

He stands up and walks towards the balcony so that his back faces me.

"She left. She's a bitch."

"Just like that. Like wind."

"At McDonald's. She said she couldn't take it anymore—all this American stuff. She needed to understand Russia again." He turns around and tries on a lopsided grin; then rubs his crotch with his right hand. Walks up to the stereo and puts on some Smashing Pumpkins. Bangs his head from side to side. "That's right! I met her through you, didn't I? I had forgotten all about that."

He slouches about the room, mumbling over the music to himself ... "She was great, man, she was fucking the thing, her tits, I tell you, I used to suck them all night." Locking his fingers together, he bends them backwards until his face contorts. Then he stops and stands there holding the pose, arching his eyebrows. "It was better then, wasn't it Godunev? Those days, the early 90s. Before everyone went mad. I could just walk down the street and pick up a girl. They were, like, into us then, we were the White Gods, the Americans. And it was so fucking cheap—I remember going to the Restaurant Prague before they closed it down and having a whole meal, including caviar, with this chick, for five dollars or something like that." He gets carried away, it's the vodka I'm sure. "These days you have all these MBAs right out of Wharton or Harvard coming here, with full expat packages. They have no idea what it was like then." He can go on like this for a while, I'm sure. I want to stop him before it becomes pathetic. So I go up to him and kiss him on the forehead.

"I love you, Kirk. But you should know that I'm living with her now."

His knuckles make a cracking sound.

"But she said she wasn't going to see anyone else. That she wanted to be alone for a while." He searches my face for an answer.

"I don't know what she told you. She's a woman, after all. You can never trust those bitches."

"She's changed?"

"She's a model these days."

He crumples his hand into a fist and brings it upwards. "I knew it. I knew it. She couldn't have stayed sweet for that long. She used to get excited just going to the Moosehead Bar and eating chicken wings.

"You know I'd love to write a feature about this, about Russian girls.

How they all want to become models. They smell like teen spirit for a year and then it's over ... they're sluts." He goes up to his bookshelf and rustles around there. "Perhaps I can pitch it to a men's magazine like Details or Esquire. Freelance something interesting for a change."

This resolve on his part seems to cheer him up. He pours another shot and hands it to me. "To Irina. Let's drink."

"I'd like you to meet her," I tell him later. "What do you think?" He doesn't seem to hear, just gazes out the window, his fingers drumming out the tune on his thighs.

"There's a huge party I'm organizing. It'll have drive. You should come."

He snaps to attention at the word party; his eyes bulge out of his face when he turns to me. It's a Moscow thing; I've seen it before. You can interrupt plans for a contract killing even with the word 'party.' Everyone just stops what they're doing and turns to you agog, licking the underside of their lower lips in anticipation.

"Party? Huh! Where? Is that Sasha Momonov involved?" he says very fast.

I wave a dismissive hand in the air. "No, this is something I'm doing with a banker. Lots of models from Red Stars, some Joe Fellacio teenagers, the whole gang. It's going to be in this Mosenka building under construction."

He nods mellow in my direction; shakes my hand vigorously. "I'll be there, man. Cool."

Very casual, he adds, "Where is it again?"

"I'll send an invitation later. But you need to write it up, front page. I'm making a debut as a party promoter here in Moscow, and I want some coverage. Spin it if you like as the evolution of the New Russian party scene. No longer cheesy with smoke machines and bad singers like Shura or Kirkoriev. We're going New York chic these days."

"Cool, man, whatever." He gives me a big, fake smile, shakes his head a bit again.

"You sure?"

"I'm sure, man." He does neck exercises as he speaks. "As I said, I'm trying to move in that direction, write about the nightlife, youth culture. Not about corruption in the Moscow city government, but closer to the pulse of Moscow. The paper needs that, it's getting stuffy these days. The eXile has really made that obvious to even the editors."

I was so green then. Thought the Moscow Times was a paper of record. Imagined that an article there might be a plus with the crowd. Whatever. I'm getting numb again, boredom creeping into the Saturday afternoon, when I remember the girl. I have left her at a café nearby, thinking I might give her a call later if the mood is right.

I snap my fingers in his face. "I've got a present for you," I say, standing up, doing the twist with the shades and the pendant. "You're going to love her."

He perks up, arches his eyebrows. "You've got a girl for me."

"Not just a girl, a girl who looks just like Irina. She's a carbon copy. Some think they're twins."

"You're kidding, right!"

"Masha's just like her. You'll see." I page her quickly, 'come immediately,' and then sit back against the couch. This I think is going to be fun.

There's a part of me that hopes it works out between them. I have this soft spot for Masha from Ivangorod. She does resemble Irina, luscious hazel hair, big shoulders, the same sensual-looking face. But just because she's not as gorgeous, her lips are thinner, she slouches a bit, her ass is bigger and misshapen on closer inspection, she's stuck on the B-list. Forced to work as a $100 whore, have the odd fling with the occasional New Russian who's going down, feeling a bit hard on his luck. She's smarter than Irina, in fact, shyer in some respects, likes to quote Mayakovsky and Tsvetaeva over mint tea, gets all romantic when I take her out to El Dorado, and tries hard to make good conversation. Poor thing.

While we're waiting, he leans over, more confident. "Listen, I've got a favor to ask, Vlada. Was there a coup a few weeks ago? I've heard rumors Yeltsin's cronies tried to dissolve Parliament after they declared the Belovezh accords illegal, so they had an excuse to postpone the elections. They almost went through with it but Chubais and the others intervened at the last minute. Did you hear about it?"

"Yeah, but it was a bit more complicated. Chubais and the reformers planned the coup, brought Yeltsin around to their side, and then cancelled it later so they'd look good. It was a cynical move on their part, to gain some popularity. There was a deal with Zyuganov, the Communist leader, that if things did succeed, they'd make him Prime Minister. Appease him and then cancel the elections." I smile smug, lean back on the couch. "In Russia, the truth is always more devious than the rumor, and more fantastic than the conjecture." Salminsky had told me that recently.

"Really. That's wild. I thought it was just Korzhakov and the gang."

"They're out, history. He'll fire them all soon. Just wait and see."

"No way, where did you hear that? From one of the oligarchs? You friends with them these days?" But I just put a finger to my lips when I hear the elevator click in the hall outside. "Just forget about work for a while. Enjoy this."

A thought strikes me. I turn to him. "Remember her face when you hit her. It becomes a bit like Mother Theresa's, radiates peace."

His expression hardens; he turns towards me, and stares silently for a while. This is what happens with Americans I remember. You reach some sort of limit and when you cross that they turn opaque, inflexible; willing to forsake everything that's passed before for some unshakeable moral certainty. Fools!

"That's wrong, Godunev. That's very wrong. In three years I never touched her, not once." His declaration adds character to his face; gives him mojo. Did she hit you, though, I want to ask (I'm almost sure she did), but the bell rings, cutting off the moment.

He gets up, gives me an expectant look, and walks towards the door. I'm afraid that he might fuck it up now.

But when he tiptoes in behind her, I realize everything's klassna. He's a bit spastic, motions towards the couch, is about to sit down next to her, changes his mind, and pulls up a chair. I've been cruel, I've made her wear her hair like Irina does, bangs falling across the forehead. She's also got on oodles of lipstick to hide the thinness of her lips. She does in fact in the dim light of his apartment resemble Irina more than I imagined.

"Privet," he says.

"Privet." She smiles at the hardwood floor, doesn't look up.

He's become all tongue-tied, keeps turning to me for a cue.

"Kirk's a great journalist. He travels all across Russia, was in Kalmykia recently. He knows more about this place than we do."

She fixes her big eyes on him. "Really. That's very interesting."

He shrugs, mouths a few words, and then goes quiet again.

"Vodka? Let's do another shot. To friendship."

After another shot, he revives. Turns to her bashful. "You want a Big Mac?"

"Big Mac? You have one here?"

"I have one in the fridge. I'll get you one."

"OK. I can have one. I didn't have breakfast this morning."

"I'm going," I say, standing up, stretching. "I have to meet some DJs for this bash. But I'll see you soon I'm sure."

"Stay here," I whisper into Masha's ear, before I leave. "Rape him if you have to."

minus fifteen

I discovered Masha, Irina's double, in an alley near Lubyanka, hiding herself behind the Doric columns of a disbanded customs house, screening her eyes from the headlights with her cupped palm. The other whores were crowded around the Mercedes, flashing their red plastic minis or tight black T-shirts with Dolce & Gabbana emblazoned across the chest, their smiles—full-lipped, brittle and forced in the frigid cold of the courtyard—a parody of New Russian seductiveness. I couldn't stand that, never could. It makes me melancholic for Russia, slightly sad, and I'd turn away, scanning the line for the naif, the Irina sprawled against the floor of the Kursky vokzal, the accidental whore.

That night it was Masha, sweet, romantic, so frozen from the winter night that she cried when hot water gushed out the bathroom taps. (I fucked her in the tub, her head pushed beneath the faucet, water flowing in rivulets down her dark hair.) Other nights there were others, some gorgeous, some just plain. I'd go for the ambitious Ukrainian girls sometimes, with high asses and rashes on their belly. The ones who realized they'd be better off slouching on the streets of the capital than waitressing in Yalta or Simferopol. I didn't ram them most times, just sat back and listened to them talk. Boast about their small apartment near Chisti Prudy, diss their first Moscow boyfriend who slept with a knife under his pillow and woke up blabbering at night. "Some of the men here, you'd never imagine what they're like. They're like wolves," they'd tell me, and I'd just smile enigmatically, give them the Godunev look.

I could have had any of the shiny club babes, the model wanna-bes, the Mausoleum girls with their belly-button rings and Wella-conditioned hair. Especially now that the parties had evolved into gatherings of the beau monde. Everyone wanted to be at our decadent bashes, hosted in buildings under construction: the Mossenka towers near Pavlovsky Vokzal; the steel-and-cobalt Central Bank building; the Menatep extension. Some of the gangsters—pathetic perestroika characters for the most part, still proud of their battle scars from the great mob wars of the early 90s—paid a thousand dollars for a party card, guaranteeing them free admission. Just so they could huddle in the sauna with their whores and do lines off their asses.

But I didn't want the golden youth. I didn't need their davai davai enthusiasm, their gadget talk and name-dropping. I craved something rawer, crazier, Moskva-Petushki-like; a self-destructive creature from within the inferno of Russia, hovering close to the flames. The first time I did the circuit was when Irina left on what I then believed was her monthly trip to Saratov. A Playboy photographer took me on the route: it was fun and frothy, just some diversion after all the champagne drunk at the opening of the Rambo Club. What are we doing, what are we doing, better to poke a hole in the wall and bang away, I kept saying. But the girl I brought home had scars across her back, gash marks like fish scales, and when I read her a poem after sex, Tsvetaeva's "Ophelia in Defense of the Danish Queen," she started to sob, quiet at first. Then she stood up and mutilated herself, gashing a knife across her belly, begging me to lick the blood.

Soon it became an addiction. I'd stand there at the clubs, pure, placid, not even jiggling in the Godunev style; just energizing the crowd with my inner radiance. And then I'd disappear, leave Irina to her model friends and agents from Red Stars, and head out into the night. Kicking the girl out just before she arrived, exhausted, smelling of money. "Godunev," she'd say, "Where were you?" And I know that she smelled the cheap Java perfume wafting across the bed in our hip new pad near Kievskaya, but she didn't say a thing. Just lay down and waited for me to let her go down on me. I had stopped hitting her and that's all she cared about then. Poor thing. She wanted so much just to preserve the illusion so she could move forwards. While I went backwards, back in time to the Russia I had known, where feelings were so close to the surface, you could taste their excreta. They tasted like shrimp.

Tonight's different, though. I'm not so sure I'm in control this time. I want to yabber jabber, shove it all out, let the words loose and watch them disappear inside someone's rich inner life. It's not going to be easy, not at all. This time I need someone who understands the insecurity behind vanity; who, in that peculiar Russian way, can see through the whole human charade. And still laugh at the apparition. So I'm going, still riding around after three hours, first the ring road, then Tverskaya, Byeloruskaya, Stoleshnikov Peroulek, but still nothing. Just tarts, vapid, eager for a buck. I even stop the cab and dash into the underpass near Pushkin. But they're horrible there, gathered in clumps like weeds, whistling at passers-by. When I emerge, a lone whore on a horse cantering down the street gives me a wave.

The vice is tightening around me: I followed Irina one Friday afternoon to the airport. She had been returning flush from her trips to Saratov, Nina Ricci perfumes in her handbag, a red Hermes scarf, Moschino leather pants. "There's new stores there," she'd say. "Even there, there are New Russians." But I wasn't so sure. I shouldn't have cared, but I did. And so once I jumped into a cab and rode after her, to Sheremetyevo I, where she boarded a plane, not to Saratov, but to Riga, Latvia. I couldn't follow her because Russians need a visa to visit those ex-Soviet Baltic countries, which think they're part of Europe now.

But the next month I did. Got Masha Tsigal to dress me up as a Delphin transvestite, cherry wig, llame dress, Japanese paper fan, and checked in behind her. Sat two rows behind her on the sleek TransAero Boeing, gulping Chablis the whole way, feeling self-conscious. It was silly, others stared at me, thought I was famous, whispered among themselves. They must have surmised I was one of those avant-garde performers who come on at the glam clubs late at night. Irina was more stylish in a black Dior skirt; I'd hear snippets of her conversation with an American seated besides her. They were discussing stock prices. LUKoil's going to go through the roof. The market's still got a lot of upside. It's performing better than the Nasdaq. It was impressive. I was sweating so much, some of the makeup started to run, mixed in with the wine and made me giddy.

In the passport line, I overheard her making a date with him for later that evening. "Vincents," he suggested, and she just did the Ira thing, nodded quietly, lifted her shades, mouthed something, and then breezed past him. I loitered around for a while, took a taxi to her hotel, the SAS Radisson. (She had mentioned it numerous times during her conversation. She was proud, I could tell, that she was booked there.) I checked in also, this time sans wig, braving their suspicious glances, eager just to go up to the room and take a long hot shower, wash away the artifice.

I want to tell someone all about this, the trip, so I'm still searching, motoring around the dark alleyways. Ah, there, I see her, standing with others near the Master & Margherita restaurant on Patriarshky Prudy. A Ptyuch girl, hair in ponytails arched over her head, a teddy-bear backpack slung around her. She has an expectant look as if she's holding something back. "I designed this myself," she tells me when I ask her to flip open her jacket, revealing a green macramé leotard with black lace extensions. "I designed myself," I say, and she becomes serious, blushes. That's the kind I like, the ones who are still waiting to feel. They stand out there, hours and hours, freezing, storing up emotions; and when someone like me comes along, they turn so emotional, you can plunge a knife through their heart and they'll thank you for the gesture.

I can feel her senses peaking as we ride around aimlessly, focusing their energies upon me. "Bite me harder," she whispers. "I like it when men are strong." So I bite her again, almost drawing blood, dig my nails into her thighs. "I like you," she says. "I really like you." But she doesn't look at me and stares out the window instead.

Her face isn't round like most; it's oval. Energy concentrates near her mouth, which quivers now as her excitement rises. Her lips are full and flat, but I don't want to kiss them. I want to draw more and more out of her, take her to a place where nothing exists apart from me. "I'm so lonely and confused," I tell her, "I just want to talk." And I tell her about my trip to Riga, following Irina there, the chain of events, while we drive around the ring road, slow, because of all the traffic and slush.

"I follow her the next morning, into Riga's Old Town, and what does she do but go straight into this bank—Parex it was called—and comes out an hour later with a Samsonite suitcase. Straight away I knew it was the dollars of our mutual friend Salminsky. It was obvious from the way she held it in front of her that it wasn't her money; it was just something she was doing for something else."

"So what did you do?"

"Nothing. I went into one of these restaurants they have there, where waitresses wear traditional Baltic costume, wood everywhere, fifty different kinds of food—and I drank vodka. Not even our Moskovskaya or Kristall, but some Latvian vodka. Tasted of fish. I just sat there, four, five hours, like a homeless person. Didn't think anything, just sat. View from the window was very pretty, their opera house was visible; like Brandenburg Gates it looks, chariots over the entranceway. And then when I was so drunk I felt light, thought I could fly over the room, I went back to the hotel. Reception, they treated me like I was some freak, yet condescended to inform me she was in the pool, so I went there. What do I see? But right there, in the changing room, is our American from the plane. Like a young Richard Gere. It's not a compliment, just obvious he thinks he's a star. No, his body wasn't that great, freckles all over his skin, so white. Americans, their skin is different from ours, you feel you pinch it and blood comes out. It's like paper, their skin. I follow him into the sauna a few minutes later ... there's nobody there ... and straight away I go up to him, stand over him, and put a finger to his forehead. He jerks back. 'I'm going to kill you,' I tell him in Russian.

"What does he do?"

"Nothing. He just stares at me, forces a smile. I know that I don't look like a gangster. Then brings his face close to mine. 'This is the Radisson, he replies in English, 'This is Latvia, It's a civilized country. Not like Russia.' I tell him. 'Remember what happened to your American colleague Paul Tatum. Shot just outside his hotel in Moscow. The same thing's going to happen to you.' But he doesn't flinch. Not even scared. Something happens to Americans when they leave Russia. They're not such cowards as they are here. So I hit him fast over the head. Not so hard, but just enough so he stands up quick. Imagine what he does. He bares his teeth and then spits at me. Of course I duck fast. When I come back up, am considering strangling him, grabbing his penis—it's circumcised, like with all Americans—when I realize I've seen him in Moscow. At one of our parties. He had tried to pass me a Benjamin so he could get into the VIP room. Thought he was so cool. Was wearing a red Octopus suit. Same second I recognize him, he does too. Does a double-take, narrows his eyes."

"I also know you," says the girl. "You're Godunev, aren't you? I know you organize parties."

I take her small hand and squeeze it. Then I bite her on the ear so hard she gasps.

"So what happened then?" she asks quietly.

"'You're Godunev?' he asked suddenly, relaxing his pose, stepping back a bit. 'Yeah, sure, the one and only,' I said, shrugging, acting chill. 'The one who throws those great parties?' 'Da, that's me.' The sycophant, he shook my hand, smiling so wide I could see the silver fillings in his teeth, and switched to Russian. 'This must be all some misunderstanding. I admire what you doing in Moscow. You've got the best parties, the best girls. It's fantastic being there. What can I do for you?' I went closer to him, noticed he had this strange habit of flicking his head back every once in a while to hide his nervousness. So I mimed his head gestures, grinned. 'Leave my girl alone.'

"'Which girl?' he starts. 'Oh, her!' He gives me a quick look, he wants to show me he's fucked her before he apologizes, but I don't let him. I just turn away and pour some water on the stones so that the heat scalds us. He's been here for a while, in the sauna, and he wants to leave, but I won't let him. I watch his paperish skin turn redder, imagine him on top of her, ... and then it's a joke. A big joke. Who cares? 'Does she give good head?' I ask him, and he wants so bad to leave, he's irritable. 'We weren't so intimate. I already said I'm sorry.' 'OK, buddy,' I say, standing up, 'you want to come to the parties, you want to be sorry, you stay here another five minutes,' and throwing some more water on the kiln I left. Watched the poor fellow through the glass door, sitting there, huddled, rubbing the sweat off his body. They're all like that, these yuppies, you have some power, they're licking your ass. We should just shoot all of them, send them back to America.

"No, that's nothing. He's nobody, some sexpat. Why I am so jittery? So jittery, Lara. Because I gave up my strength in Riga. My roof flew away there, in Latvia. Like a rocket. Whoosh. How? I'll tell you. Of course, I slapped her in the swimming pool. She's such a fool, she hugged me first, thinking it's him when I dived in and grabbed her ass underwater. I was so enraged then that I hit her, right there, in front of everyone, and pinched her ass. And then she said, 'I'll explain everything, everything. I love you, Godunev.'

"So we went to some restaurant, wandered like lovers afterwards, admiring the caryatids on the buildings there, kicking cobblestones, ducking through archways. Try to imagine what happens to us Russians when we're in Europe, some small European town. Even Riga. We forget everything about our Moscow arrogance. We become fools, romantic, Prince Myshkins. In Moscow, we never speak to each other almost, and here we're quoting Pushkin. There, there's such small streets, gas lamps, wrought-iron gates, and people so silent, like the snow, that you become soft. 'I never slept with Peter,' she says, and I believe her. We drink Merlot in the 'Black Monk', some kind of mediaeval place, and she suggests, 'Let's take some money for ourselves. Salminsky will never know. I'm the owner of the Alphabeta Company in Cyprus. He just sends the money there and then they wire it to Riga. It's the only way they can get hard currency into Russia, through this back door. Such big sums of money, six million, ten million dollars. What is half a million?'

"So there. We went to the same bank on Monday and deposited the cash. 'For our future,' she said. I had agreed, such a durak I am. And now back here, Moscow, I feel like the Caucasian Prisoner. They are just waiting and waiting, and then something will happen. Like with that Georgian from Paris. Nothing. It's not for you.

"Boo," I shout into her ear. "Boo. Just like that." I blow into my cupped palm. "I could be memory." She holds me tight against her as we clamber up the half-finished stairs of the Mossenka building. It's my idea, to creep into here at night. I still remember the door codes from having thrown the bash here last month. "Let's go to the top and watch our spit go into freefall," I had suggested as we passed it. Now we're here, and it's pitch-black in parts, me using a lighter to lead the way. Whoa.

Other times city light comes streaming through exposed windows, their panes haphazardly covered with tinted glass. It's a cheesy building, neo-classical empire style in the front facing the street, with Doric columns and high friezes; glass-and-steel in the back, which faces the bridge. The roof surmounted with a Russian cupola, a bell tower, painted green and orange.

During the tusovka, all us VIPs gathered in the hidden chambers between the floors, the half-floors, where the saunas and the casinos and the bedrooms with VCRs and mini-bars are concealed from the public. There's secret doors on the landings of the stairway which lead there; low spaces just six feet high, stacked between the main floors. Outside, on the main landings, there were DJs spinning tracks, a fashion show by Masha Leontyevo, some B-grade models hanging around, dressed like pirates with patches over their eyes and exposed breasts tattooed with the skull and crossbones. But inside, just below them, we were gathered. I had had someone throw silk fabric all over the place so that it was cosy, layers of cloth everywhere, hanging from the ceiling. There were Oriental rugs on the floor, divans strewn about, and fast-food cartons in a side room, with cocaine, ecstasy, mushrooms, joints … everything.

I banged the twins in the sauna, I remember, just before midnight. The older one, prettier than her twin, hadn't wanted to. "It's the night before Easter," she begged. "Jesus hasn't risen yet. We're still fasting. Just wait till midnight." But I had gotten her high on a joint and Viagra cocktails, and thrown her against the wooden bleachers. Just seconds after

I came, the church bells tolled. Isus Voskres, Istinu Voskres. They had both lain there, satiated and confused from the drugs. The younger one, her feet on the cold stones of the kiln, watched me, her pupils dilated. I had bent closer, put a hand between her legs, preparing her for a second attempt, when she jumped up, bursting into tears. "We've committed a sin. God's never going to forgive us. Aihee, what are we going to do?"

Irina let Salminsky eat her out that night. I'm sure of that. She got like that when she was high, wanted to stand with her back against a common wall, her right leg up against a loose brick or metal pylon, and roll her eyes when they dived under her skirt. It was a pleasure I sometimes denied her. Out of pride. But Salminsky didn't care—he was crazy about her. Desperate to possess her, however he could. He had made her the owner of Alphabeta as a bribe, I think, showered other gifts upon her in the past. For all his efforts, though, he'd never give her a sleepless night. His problem was that he didn't know how to deny women things, to keep them second-guessing, play with their expectations. Instead he just gave and gave, more and more, so much that they stopped respecting him. Treated him as something to be taken for granted, closing their eyes when he fucked them, while fantasizing about the muscular driver with the missing front tooth instead.

"Why, why?" he asked me once at the fag end of our second bash. "I gave that girl Vika a Volvo and the keys to an apartment near Tverskaya, and still, *bilyaet*, she follows some club kid around like a cheap whore." I pinched his ears—it was a habit I had developed with him—and whirled around a bit. "Women are like blini. You have to keep them warm." Talk to them I should have said. Remember when you were seventeen and you sat by the Lenin monument at dusk and alluded to your old man's porno collection. Or just stroked their hair and got all misty-eyed. We're not too old for that, not yet. But of course he wouldn't have understood. "Godunev," he'd have said, "you're such a stupid romantic. Men like you should be sent to dig a road through the Altai mountains. Sing a song and watch the birds."

"Where does all the money come from?" I had asked him then, imagining he might confess. I had understood that the parties at least were designed to attract tenants to the new buildings, get them so drunk and high it'd be easier to fleece them the next morning. But that's all I knew. It was his turn to twist my ears. "Dollars. You want to know where we find them? I'll tell you." He pinched his large nose with his right hand and pulled it forward. "Buratino. You remember him? He gives us all this wealth, he just loves us. We share the same long nose." And then he kissed me on the left ear. A big wet kiss.

The girl leans out the window on the top floor and points an arm at the spires of the Kremlin. "You know what I want? I want to fly. Like Woland. I want to spread my arms and soar above this city, watch my reflection in the Patriarshky ponds. Howl into the night so all my girlfriends look up from the headlights, turn their faces to the stars for once."

"You're crazy."

"You're also not normal." She comes up to me and touches me between the eyes with her thumb. You're just spoiled because all the girls love you; you're so relaxed, so confident. Like a rich poet. Of course, they don't exist any more in our Russia. Our poor Russia.

"Why are you with me? Why not with Irina, or with some other model?" She giggles, puts a hand over her mouth to hide her mirth, and then hugs me suddenly. "Leave her. We'll be together, for ever. Like Romeo and Juliet."

I'm not sure what I want—not this I think—so I start to push her away gently. She sobs, walks backwards, and leans against an arch under the cupola.

"Tell me what to do. I'll do it."

"Remember Botticelli's Venus, her arms raised in the air. Rising out of that lotus. I want you to undress and stand like a ballerina, your arms above your head."

Her skin is milky white, a big mole on her left ass cheek, nearer the thigh. Her breasts smallish, as I like, nipples pert like acorns. I go up to her and put a hand on her cunt. It's wet. "Tell me a story," I say, rubbing her labia. "Something bad." She thinks for a while and then goes aah.

"You know what happened to me the other night? I went home with this man, Georgian or Armenian I think, not bad, dressed in a suit, very serious. We go back to his apartment, in the center, everything'll be all right, I think. But inside there's eight other men waiting for me. Eight men, all from the Caucasus, and not like him at all. Dressed in cheap track suits. They're all drunk, leering at me, touching me as soon as I walk into the room."

I'm still stroking her, increasing the pace as her excitement rises. "What happened then?"

"No, what happened? I was scared in the beginning, thought they might try to kill me, scar me with a knife at least. It happened with one of our girls, they gashed her all over her back."

"And..."

"Nothing. They were quite normal in fact, just wanted to fuck me. Touch me everywhere. I was there for five hours and then they let me go. Gave me a ram's horn as a parting gift. I was so happy to leave, went to the Starlite Diner and had a strawberry milkshake. Even read the Moscow Times, though I didn't understand much."

She's getting more excited, pushing down to make contact with my hand. I bunch three fingers together and slide them in.

"Now that I think about it, it was great," she continues. "So many men, they all wanted me, they all thought me beautiful. That's also a high, just being wanted by so many men, so horny, so hungry, and I gave them pleasure, some happiness. Poor men, hadn't been with a woman in months, I think. You understand me?" she asks. "You understand me, you rich poet."

After she comes, we lie against the wooden floor. The poor Turks, they come here to Moscow to work, to make their buck, praying to their Gods at noon, shutting out the din of the cranes overhead. Gepetto, I think. I'm like him, bringing us all to life. Breathing something into their lives which they didn't realize existed before. There's a vein under my forehead which goes tic-toc sometimes, and now it's shut off, quiet. I just hold her close; her face is still wet from all the tears, and it makes me calm. Lara, I repeat, Lara. She turns to me, has a strange look in her eyes.

"You know something, Godunev?" she says, her voice halting. "I've been thinking about all this you said, and I'm sure that Ira knew you had followed her in advance. She also knows Masha Tsigal, I think; it's quite possible she was warned. She's just using you, Vlad, trying to draw you into her life, so you can't escape."

I grab her ass and squeeze it hard. "Rubbish. She didn't even notice me in the plane, was busy with her own plans. She's not so smart as you think, just a provincial girl."

"I know women, you Russian men are always underestimating us." But I just put a hand over her mouth and shut her up. I stroke her hair, rub my hand down her back, and then, propping myself up on an elbow, slide downwards, spreading her legs, and sticking my nose there, between her. It smells so strong, so pungent, all thoughts, worries are wiped out . I could stay here for hours, I think, sticking a tongue out.

I hear the sounds first: the muffled shouts and the banging of doors; the static of walkie-talkies. I shake the girl. "What's going on?"

"Nichivo, let's sleep some more. I'm so tired."

"Wait, something's going on." I slide over to the window and peer out. It faces the canal and St. Basil's beyond, so I can't see much, just the cars driving out the Baltschug. I lean out further and crane my neck for a view of the entrance. The voices are louder out in the air, I can even hear the stamping of boots. "Hold me," I shout at her, and slither out over the window frame even further, so I can see the high antenna and sleek roof of what must be a Range Rover. STIRLITZ! Berezhovsky's boys. Bilyaet! I can imagine what happened. We must have triggered an alarm on the way up, bringing them here in a jiffy. They're going to comb the building from the first floor up, and when they find us, one of them might shoot. They're former KGB brutes. A friend of ours died like that the other week, shot leaving his own bank late one night.

These thoughts go through my head in a fraction of a second, and then I'm down on my knees, searching frantically for the mobile. I call both the deputy head of RUOP and the vice mayor of Moscow, but there's no answer. The owner of the Mausoleum nightclub is in a sauna. "Berezhovsky's men?" he asks. There's a long pause. "Call Salminsky. Other than Berezhovsky, he's the only one who can do anything." So I dial the number. I can't care at this moment that we haven't spoken for more than a week. Already I can hear them banging against the walls below.

The girl's shaking me. "What's going on? What have we done?"

"Security," I tell her. "They have guns."

She runs to the window and climbs up on the ledge. "It's better if I jump now. I know these men, they're wolves. I've slept with some of them. They can do anything, even torture us."

"Stop screaming. Shut up." I grab her as she struggles against me and push her against the wall. "They'll hear us and come right away. I'll call someone. Everything'll be OK." With one hand around her mouth, I call him. A girl picks up the phone.

"Haallyooo." It's the older twin. I recognize her voice immediately.

"Olga, it's Godunev, give Yuri the receiver. It's urgent."

"Why?" Her voice is playful. "He's playing billiards. He's about to win. What are you doing? Enjoying some freebie as usual?" I'm losing patience. "Olga, this isn't time for jokes. I'm caught up in a sweep. They can kill me if you don't call him."

She laughs into the phone. "That's an answering strike from God, perhaps. You remember what happened with us?"

I've got to keep my cool. "Drugs are to blame. Not me. I was their slave."

"Da! You're so slick. OK, I believe you. Noh, what'll you give me if I call him?"

"I'll leave you both alone forever."

"You promise?"

"Of course. It's my word."

When Salminsky comes on the line, he's livid. "Hide," he says. "What else can I advise? Go and conceal yourself under the sauna. They'll never find you.

"Use your charm," he says after a while. He just grunts when I tell him they're getting closer. "OK, I'm coming. I'll place a call. But remember, it's for Irina. You don't deserve her."

He calls five minutes later. "Start walking downstairs. Everything's in order. I'm waiting for you outside."

"Everything OK," says the girl. She's got a doe-eyed expression now, her eyes aglow with dried tears. She shakes her head. "You always know what to do."

I hang my hands at my side, open and close them into fists. "Yeah, sure. Got some friends, that's all." I hate her now because of her comments about Irina. So I glance at my watch, and then point to the dial with my finger.

"Wait here. I'll be back in five minutes."

"Promise?"

"Of course. Just got to make sure everything's OK."

Once outside, I lock the door leading down to the stairs from the outside. It's got a bolt, an old-fashioned one, in place. Then I hop down the stairs, two or three at a time. It's all fine I think. I'll make up something for Salminsky, and we'll be on our way.

A few landings down though, someone emerges out the darkness and whacks me over the neck so I come crashing down.

"Found you, like a rat. Oleg always know how to catch them, the thieves. We're going to have some fun now." He kicks me in the ribs, once, twice, pushes the cold end of something metallic against the back of my head. "Who are you?"

"Everything's in order. My friend called your boss. It's all a misunderstanding."

"You spies all know how to talk. No-one told me anything. Oleg doesn't change his mind like that."

He reaches down and pulls the wallet from my leather pants. Switches on a flashlight; I can now see the lattices in the marble floor. I can hear him flicking through the wallet, pulling out the dollars, stuffing them in his pocket.

"Turn around."

He's wearing black Gore-Tex tights, a thick dun army sweater, a box of Marlboro sticking out the arm pocket. His brow is sharp, angular, declivities on either side above the sideburns. His nose is flat like a bulldog's. "Nu, chto?"

I know that if I falter for an instant it might be the end. So I get into a sitting position as quick as I can, despite the pain in the ribs, and spit at him.

"You don't know who I am. Berezhovsky? He's my friend. Vlad Yevstasief, his business partner, we go the sauna together. We had a business party here two weeks ago, you must have heard about it. I just came to get some things that were left behind. You want to check, call downstairs. They'll tell you it's all in order."

He cocks his Kalashnikov and rubs the barrel against my right ear. "You don't have to speak so fast." He does an imitation of a Moscow accent, vowels emphasized, consonants silent at the end. "I'm from Krasnoyarsk, Sibiiir; all you Moscow people, I could shoot you like dogs."

"Harasho. I'll tell you where your boss is right now."

This gives him pause. "Where is he?"

"In London. In the Park Lane Hotel. The King Edward Suite."

He shuts one eyes, stares at me out the other. Still watching me restlessly, he presses the button on the walkie-talkie.

"Seryosha. Oleg here."

"Everything's OK. He's one of ours. I see."

He takes the Marlboro packet out of his arm-pocket and opens it towards me.

"Cigarette?"

"Sure."

"You see," he says, patting me on the shoulder, "it's our work. Until we check someone out we can't relax. You understand that, don't you? It's our training, every day is like war for us."

He bares his teeth, does a good imitation of a laugh. "In Russia, there are two problems: fools and roads." I laugh along with him. Hee, hee, he laughs some more. Wipes his brow. Waits for me to say something but I don't. He expects me to ask for the cash back but it's not important. It was just a couple hundred dollars. I'm already moving towards the door.

"I'll take you down."

I hold a hand up. "Upstairs there's a girl. Very beautiful. Free her after five minutes. And give her some of my dollars."

"You don't understand," says Salminsky when we're safe in the back seat of his Mercedes 600. "There's a war going on. Berezhovsky versus Gusinsky. They're going to rip each other apart, just for this Svyazinvest sale. Our Berezhovksy has the ear of Tanya, but still, everyone's tense, like ice about to melt. One match and there'll be a big shoot-out. You don't have to get involved in all this. You live, like, like, you're in New York or London. This is Russia!!! Moskva!! You understand."

I smile weakly. "It's all clear. Thanks for coming so quick."

He puts his face close to mine. "What were you doing there? Jerking off? Why? At this time of night. Where's Irina?"

There's a sheen to his face, his cheeks are taut, fresh. I can tell he's just had someone killed. He gets like this after he's ordered a contract killing, all giddy and confident.

"Fuck you. Whom did you give to Hades today? I have intuition. I can tell these things. I'm still in control, despite what you might think." I've done a line of coke off a little spoon before emerging, and I'm high, want to show him up. "You know what I did today. I was in line at this shop, just buying a pack of cigarettes, and there was this old babushka there, ahead of me. 'How much are those apples?' she had asked, pointing at some rotting fruit in a basket by the side. 'Five roubles,' the salesgirl said, and she shook her head. 'Five roubles, so much just for apples.' So I bought two kilos of fresh apples and ran after her when she left the shop. Handed them to her. 'Here, for you,' I said, 'be happy.' She kissed me on the hands, crossed herself. 'God bless you,' she said. 'Even in these times, there are some human beings around.'"

He presses my shoulders, gives me a weird look. "You're high, Godunev, sweating. What's wrong with you? You're going to go under if you continue like this, and that old lady isn't going to save you either. Just be cool, like you used to be." He snaps his fingers in the air. "I'm a biznisman, you forget. Not a killyer." He points at his Hermes tie. "I just came from work. We're working on this new privatization." He turns quiet though and rolls down the tinted window. Sits there and sniffs the cold air. Shakes his head. "Russia. You can live here hundred years and still have no idea what's going on. This is a land of miracles."

"One day a man is breathing, sitting constipated in the toilet, cursing his wife. Next day he's as dead as the Sea of Azov. That's life here these days. Why you came back? Better to sit in America and think about Russia than to sit here and dream about America. There people understand only what they need to. A scientist spends ten years on one problem—but they still pay him every month. Here! We can't even imagine next year, but in ten years we'll be just like Europe, Paris or London? What you think, Godunev? We'll all be civilized in ten years?"

"Our tennis certainly won't be longer in ten years. I can bet it'll be all shriveled up."

"Vot, sex. You're always coming straight to the point. Where are we going tonight?"

There's still this excruciating pain in my chest. "Home. I'm almost a dead man."

"What you talking about? The night is young. The twins have given me some energy. Where's Irina?"

"Mausoleum perhaps. Masha Tsigal is having some fashion show there."

"Let's go there."

"We can."

He looks at me. "You don't want." He claps his hands together. "I know. Davai Rasputin. Stalker is going to be there tonight. You know Stalker? He understands death better than any of us. He's midwifed it more than a hundred times."

One thing I had over Salminsky was an ability to project my aesthetic upon others. It makes him uncomfortable, my presence that is. He can't just turn off, as he does in the company of other New Russians, and turn to his id for pointers. With Godunev there the ante has been upped, the truth pill has been swallowed. He can't just wallow in his wealth, throw his cash around like a bandit, pretend that he's having fun. He knows that I can tell the difference between him impressing others—and him impressing himself. Sometimes, in the past, he's understood, seen the world through my eyes. He's been voguing on the floor, chilling to Kruger & Dorfmeister, the ecstasy heightening his senses, and he starts to move naturally. So sweet, so in with the vibe, that he doesn't even notice that the girl comes up and rub herself against him. She's just feeling, grooving like him, reacting to his aura—not his status. He jerks his shoulders and twists around, raises up her hand and throws her in a circle. All the while his face set in a smile so deep it can't be peeled off. He'd come to me later then, stick his tongue out and wiggle it in the air.

"I see everything at this time."

So as soon as we enter Rasputin, he throws his hands in the air. "What kind of music is this? How can we enjoy when they're playing such chy-yova."

He takes a couch near the stage and calls the manager over. "Put on something other. Something with rhythm in it. We can't relax to this pensioner music."

Then he turns to me and bares his teeth. "Let's call Stalker. He'll tell us a story."

Stalker's got an oversize bald head with small gray eyes and thin eyebrows—so blond he looks ghoulish. He's wearing a one-piece Atomic track suit with red stripes running along the sleeves and the sides of the pants. There's a scar meandering down the side of his skull, to the right ear. He's with three strippers, one with long, lamprey-shaped breasts, which she's shaking in his face.

"Tequila," he says when he comes over. "Tequila very good." But he's not drunk. It seems that Stalker can never get drunk. Even after the fifth tequila he's still as serious as a tomb. Studies me with his red-flecked steel-gray eyes and runs a hand down his cheek.

"Tell us a story. Tell us something interesting," demands Salminsky.

He pats the girl on his lap and pulls at her belly-button ring.

"I'm a man who does things. No kind of Dostoevsky or Gogol. You have a problem—I can fix it. That's all."

Salminsky snaps his fingers. "More tequila," he tells the topless waitress. "And some zakuski—blini with black caviar. Champagne also, the best. Veuve Cliquot."

He runs his hand along Stalker's pate. "You've already worked today. Tell us a story, a good one."

"Yes, yes, tell us," cries the stripper on his lap.

He closes his eyes and leans back against the leopard-skin couch.

"As I said, I'm man of action. Everything that's done is done by me and me alone. I'm like a writer or a scientist: I don't depend on intermediaries. So last week I meet this Indian man in his office. Short, quite thin, no big, what you call it, paunch, eats a lot. We sat there, one hour, two maybe, and whole time he's eating, some kind of puffs, then bread like lavash, with curry, with vegetables, chicken, everything. He talks a lot, licking his fingers with his hand, about their ancient culture, friendship between India and Russia. I just sit there, hands crossed against my chest, eyes closed. I'm man of business, I don't need all of this yak-yak. Usually people just give me name, address, and that's all. I don't need philosophy, history. That's for later, like now, when we're relaxing. No, he's serious businessman, does some kind of import-export, knows many solid people, so I sit quiet.

"At the end of it all, I open my eyes, ask him again. 'Do you have name?' That's all I need. He jumps up, shakes his hands in the air. 'No shooting, no guns.'" Stalker bends forwards and turns to us. "Do you know what he wanted? He wanted me to put some powder in the curry. Poison.

"Rudely speaking, that's the biggest insult for a professional like me. I want to be last person they see before they go for their meeting up there. All this hidden stuff not for me. People come to me because I'm honest, I'm old-fashioned maybe. But I'm efficient, I don't end up sending someone else to their fate by accident."

"You're right, of course. No, what did you do?"

"'How would you want to die?' I asked him. 'Like a rat twitching and clawing—or like a human being?'

"He became very serious, acted like he was insulted. 'That's not a correct question' he said. Then he stopped eating, turned his lips upwards, and said, can you believe this, 'I'd like you to leave. Our interview is over.'" Stalker laughs. "It's the first time someone treated me like that. Indians, they must understand that tomorrow can be different. Usually, no-one wants to be my enemy."

Salminsky claps. "Correct. Only fools do that."

He turns to me. "What you think, Godunev. How you want to die?"

I vogue a bit with my shades, raise a toast to them, but Stalker can tell I'm troubled. He intuits my fear—but not the reasons. So he whispers quick in my ear. "You want something done? Is that why you're here."

"Godunev's sad because he played tag with the Stirlitz boys today. No, that's over. He's going to treat us tonight. Aren't you Godunev?"

He gives me a piercing look, sniffs quickly as he's wont to, and I understand that he knows that I know that he knows about the dollars. I shrug. It's hard being insouciant when you've mucked around in the shit. I could kill Irina at this point. She's like Eve, I think, tempting me with the apple.

"You're familiar with the menu here, Godunev. It's a very interesting one." He picks up the velour-padded menu and starts to read from it.

"$100 for a lap dance. That's nothing. $500 for a lap dance and … something else.. with five girls. That's also common. Vot, here, $1500 to fire a stripper. What you think, Godunev. Shall we fire that girl," he says, pointing at the raven-haired girl on Stalker's lap.

"Always do things in threes. Her, and her two friends." I'm nervous now, can guess what's coming, but try to keep my cool. "These three are fired." One of them, older, transvestite-like, with big shoulders and a masculine jaw, comes up to us and puts her hands on my lap.

"You can't do this. I have a small girl, I'll have to go back to Ukraine where there's no work. I've only been working here for two weeks, what am I going to do."

"Here's a thousand dollars," says Salminsky, pulling some notes out his pocket. "Now leave quiet. We don't need yolki-palki."

That's when I notice the Richard Gere American, huddled on a couch near the back, wrapped around some sweet-looking blonde, with big, drooping eyes and narrow, exposed shoulders. He's with a group of other Americans, all dressed alike in tuxes and bow ties.

"Her," I tell the manager, pointing at his girl. "She's gone."

He wrings his hands. "That's not possible. They're big clients. We can't fire them while they're with other clients. After some time, no problem."

I stand up and run a finger along his ear in Salminsky's way. "How much? Double. Triple. Just tell us."

He just sweats, wipes his brows with a red paper napkin; little clots of paper stick to his forehead.

Salminsky starts swearing. "Kozol, pashol nachyui, bilyaet, why you need a menu then? You know what we are going to do then," he says, stabbing his finger at the menu.

"We're going to burn this place down. Here it's written that it costs $500,000. I have the money, fresh hundred-dollar bills, the new kind that were just issued a month ago," he says, pointing at a suitcase near his leg.

The manager, a short Armenian man in a cummerbund, throws his hands in the air, turns around, and walks quickly towards the boss. "I'll call Sylvester."

Stalker just sits still with his eyes closed. "I've seen this before. I've seen everything before. They have a fuse which short-circuits and sets the floor on fire. Then everything'll burn very fast." He drums his fingers against his lap. I notice that he has just four digits on his right hand. The pinkie is missing.

While we're standing outside watching the blaze, the American comes up to me.

"One of my friends was in the bathroom. He almost got caught in the fire. This is crazy—you might have at least warned us."

I put a finger to my lips and wink at him. Then I pull out a 'Godunev card' with my picture on it and hand it to him. "That's for you. For all the trouble."

He stares at me for a bit, turns the card around, and then shaking my hand quick, murmuring thanks, walks away. I watch him run to his friends, stand around proud, while they pass the card around. Losers.

Salminsky puts his arm around me, draws me closer. "Godunev, we're friends again, aren't we? We're even, aren't we?"

"What do you mean?"

"I know all about the money in Riga. The half a million dollars. There's a lot of cash sloshing around now, but we're not that stupid. So now you owe me a million. Either you get the half out of the bank, and find the rest, or you do me a favor. Which one will it be?"

I could throw up, and there's a burning in my throat. I really don't feel that relaxed any more, not tonight. A line from Pink Floyd comes to mind, two lost souls swimming ..., but I shut it out. That's the past; now is the present, the future.

"What's the favor?"

"Pinocchio wants to own the Kremlin. Our great Kremlin. But he needs your help. It's not going to be easy—not as simple as throwing a party. You're going to get involved, aren't you?"

"I don't have to kill anyone, do I?"

He exhales, watches his breath turn into frost. "It all depends how clever you are."

"We'll see." I could escape, I think, go back to wandering the world. But the hole has been dug too deep for me to clamber out of. Either I swim along with them, or I'm a dead man walking.

"You're a bastard," I rebuke him, "the worst kind." I punch him on his face, and on his chest, hiding my virulent hate and frustration behind an impish grin. When we're rolling in the snow, his eyes turn on me, watching my face for an answer.

minus twelve

Even then I realize I didn't grasp her intentions, guess at her game plan. I was mistaken in assuming she was leaving against her volition. (How could I have known that she had wished for just such a scenario for quite a while?) With corruption and capital flight having become more of an issue this spring, investigators had traced money transfers to the Alphabeta house in Cyprus—and were close to discovering the identity of its owner, i.e. Irina. It was just a matter of time, we figured, before they'd be knocking on our apartment door. So we decided to fly her off to New York before then, insulate ourselves from the risk.

There's just one last thing left to do before she flies out, a visit to her mother in Saratov. I go along with her, slightly guilty that it's come to this so soon but also harboring a secret agenda of my own which she knows nothing about. "Oh, these tea holders, aren't they divine?" she gushes on the train, admiring their copper filigree and grooved handles.

Taking a sip of the hot black tea, she wrinkles that nose of hers, still pretty, still evocative despite all that white powder shoved up its passages.

"It'll be different in America, won't it? They don't have all these traditions. Everyone drives around in cars all the time." She sighs. "I'll be alone there, Godunev. What'll I do?" There's nothing visible in the night outside, beyond the grimy windows draped with stiff red curtains. Just the kiti-kiti-kee of the engine. Kiti-kiti-kee it goes, clack, clack, as if measuring out the distance from Moscow. Irina claps her hands. "There are forests outside, they'll be silvery in the morning light. I remember when we used to take the day train, all those birch trees. You could almost touch them.

"Let's get up early and wander about the station at Tambov or some place like that."

"Malchik hochet Tambov, chiki-chiki-chiki chiki-ta. Malchik hochet Tamboooov..." I sing, my voice loud. I'm coked up again, and she knows that, she can feel it in my nervous energy. She joins along, her voice too high, and then stops when I stand up and pace the small compartment.

"Godunev," she seems to say with her eyes, but I ignore the silent appeal. Just sit back down, arms folded across my chest, and gaze out the window. The loudspeakers drone some Russian folk songs, so I stand up again and turn the knob, but the volume doesn't dim.

It's all happened a bit suddenly for her, I think. It was just last week that the tax police started to close in on Alphabeta, sent a man down to Cyprus to make inquiries. Even I didn't realize it was a funnel for earnings from Norilsk Nickel, but that's beside the point. We've arranged the visa and think it best she disappears to New York for a while. She should be overjoyed, she's been complaining about Russia for years, but instead she just sits and frets. "I have to see Mama before I leave," she'd said, so here we are, sitting in the first-class cabin of the Moscow-Astrakhan express; ignoring each other.

When I don't grasp her hand, which lies limp on the beige table between us, she calls her friends in Moscow. She's got loads of them, all young models like her, their energies focused on tomorrow's parties and fashion shows. "Olga, privet, this is Irina. I'm sitting on a train to Saratov with Godunev. It's boring here. What's happening in Moscow? Really! Bartenev is having a show at the Radisson? I wish I was there." All her conversations seemed the same, vapid and repetitive. I wanted to grab the mobile from her.

Hunching over, I try to think about Victor Pelevin, this new writer I've been reading. I've got lots of ideas—useless this new crop of writers for the most part, hologram of Yeltsin, politics as a stage—but can't focus. Time is money but money is not time, he had said when I met him once at Dusk Till Dawn's Titty-Twister party. Money is happiness and happiness is money. It's all linked, his epigrams, to the character Vitye in one of his books. That line, what did he say when we was alone among the pipes? But I can't remember.

Frustrated, I clap my fingers and mutter to myself. Pervert Datsenko, blow-up picture of a pussy above his desk. What kind of pussy? Pelevin had asked. Yes, what kind of pussy do I like. Shaved, hairy 70s pie, or one with a tongue pad. Irina's shaved, yes, that's right, all the time isn't it.

Irina strokes my hand. "Are you OK? Would you like a valium? I've got some left."

I ignore her and slouch towards the door, walk about the narrow passageway, pulling a curtain aside to gaze at the rush of lights outside. Most of the doors are closed, sounds of snoring from within, but there's one open: I hear someone cackle as I pass. I peek in out of curiosity, and there's Boris Yeltsin sitting there, I promise. He's got the same bloated pink face, the flat proud nose and the white gelled hair, his shirt's even the same, starched white and open near the neck. It's his twin, I think at first, the one they parade in front of the cameras when he's too sick to show up at the Kremlin. One of those doubles like the Albanian dictator Enver Hoxha had, trained to act and speak like him.

"Boris Nikolaevich," I mumble. Hearing me, he stands up with a shot of vodka in his hand, and toasts, "Za Boris Nikolaevich. Za Yeltsina." Dazed and confused, I join him in his toast, downing the shot he hands me. When I wipe my mouth with the back of my manicured hand—so white and smooth—he turns to me.

"Godunev?" he asks. "Don't you remember me?"

"You? I have no recollection. Was it with Salminsky somewhere?"

His eyes twinkle. He shakes his head much too fast for a Yeltsin double. "At one of your parties. I was with Lenin and Gorbachev, and ... Brezhnev was there too. It was a great evening. It was the first time no-one asked me to wave a baton around or swing a tennis racket when drunk. And the girls, what beauties. Where did you find them?"

I recall now, I realize. It was at one of our first bashes at the Bulgarian Cultural Center. We had hired out all these doubles to spice up the evening. Lenin was fun, I remember, he lay down in a coffin and had some of us spray champagne on him. And Yeltsin was depressed, that's right, just shuffling around in the corner.

"I'm from Astrakhan," he adds proudly, pointing to two young men at his side. "Going back for a while to enjoy the sea, have some real caviar. Spend the afternoons in a café reading the papers. Ah! What a relief to be outside Moscow. In that city, there are just cockroaches and bandits. And everything's so expensive. One cup of coffee at a kiosk costs one dollar. Six roubles. In Astrakhan it's one rouble.

"Sit down," he insists, making some room in the compartment. "Let's drink to Mother Russia."

"You know something," he says, after another couple shots. "I'm the last of a dying race. How much do you give me? Sixty, seventy? I have sixty nine years," he says, pulling at his grey hairs. "Most of my classmates are dead. Why?" He waves his finger in the stale air. "Not because of vodka or smoking, like everyone says. Because they lost hope. They couldn't see the light at the end. Look at me. I was an inspector at a caviar factory, like work, it was sufficient. When market reforms started some Georgian bandits took over. 'Old Daddy,' they said, 'go back to your garden.' One year later, after I wrote many letters, they gave me a pension. How much? Twenty dollars a month! Can one live on that? Even in the provinces! I helped defend Stalingrad against the Germans. And look what happens. Only in our miraculous country."

He pauses, studies me slyly, licking his tongue against his lower lip.

"What are you going to the provinces for? Organizing a party there?"

"I'm going to see my mother." It comes out so quick, it's too late to retract the confession. I just stare at him now, cursing the alcohol. He lifts his glass, speaks very slow, in a baritone, like he's really Yeltsin. "You're one of us. I thought you were a Muscovite."

I don't quite know what to say. I avert his gaze and stare at one of the young men instead. He glares at me with hostility—or is it just curiosity? He's wearing a dirty track suit, his slipper-clad feet wedged between two cheap striped plastic bags. His tireless, opaque eyes are riveted on me. A shiver runs down my spine. "It's cold in here," I mumble, and bring my arms together.

"It's not cold, there's just a draft from the corridor," says the other young man, and, reaching across me quick, shuts the door with a bang. We're all cramped in there together now, our faces garish in the weak glow from the sodium bulb above. Strange I think. Bizarre being outside Moscow. I feel I've entered another country, gone back in time and space. There, among the wide boulevards of the Sadovaya, Paris, Milan, London, seem so close, just a breath away. Almost as near as the foreign labels on our jackets. And here! I'm ashamed all of a sudden of the expensive Prada jacket, the spit-polished Hugo Boss loafers. I hide my shoes, tuck them under the bunk, make a move for the door.

"Stay," says one of them, "the bottle's not finished yet."

So I sit down again, uncertain. The old man has almost passed out, his big head lolls against the velour backrest of the train. Both of them stare at me, like I'm a television screen.

"Za Yeltsina," cheers the grandfather, waking up. He stares around him, and guffaws. "You're still here. Let's have another toast." With him I feel safer; he's part of our world. He opens and shuts his eyes; they're kind, benevolent. I trust him for no reason. I lean over and ask him quickly, before I might censor myself. "What would you think if someone bought the Kremlin?"

"What? What are you talking about?"

I wave my arms impatiently. "You know, bought the Kremlin, as they have Norilsk or Gazprom. Privatized it."

"Who? Foreigners or our Russians?"

"Whatever."

He thinks about this for a second, shakes his somber head about, and then pumps his fist in the air. "Let them do whatever they want. Stalin wasn't even Russian, and he was better than these scoundrels. Yes, let the Germans buy the Kremlin and give us the money. Then I'll die …" He tries to finish the sentence, but gasps, breathes in big gusts of air, and then falls against the shoulder of his companion.

When I'm back in our compartment, I'm relieved to see Irina again. So clean she is, her teeth white, her skin fresh and warm, the pink Jil Sander shirt just outlining the curve of her breasts. "Where were you?" she asks.

"Oh, nowhere. Just wandering around. Had some vodka with some people down there." I weave a bit as I walk and then fall against her. She ignores me, goes back to reading her British Vogue; a wayward hand strokes me tenderly across the cheek.

"What do you think of John-Paul Gaultier?" she asks shyly, after a while.

"What?"

"Gaultier! What do you think of him?"

"Oh, nothing. Latex and rubber, conical projections. Just tries to shock. Not my kind of fashion. You know what I like, classic, stylish wear. Simple fabrics, linen, velvet, cotton, leather perhaps. Straight lines, a dash of color a.k.a Paul Smith. Minimalism rather than gauche. Gold, heavy brocade, ridiculous head gear, it's fun for parties, but not for living. Some innovations like sarongs are OK. Handmade clothes in general. Shades and shoes must be top quality, a bit ostentatious. That's it." I'm impressed by my own coherence.

She protests. "But what about Alexander McQueen or even our very own Bartenev? They're taking risks, using new fabrics, stretching the limits of what's possible. That's more interesting than just classic fashion."

"But that's show business, not fashion. They want to be rock stars, they're not designers who care about their fabrics, make clothes that last years. That's more important than all this boom boom show bizness."

She gets this faraway look in her eyes, a thin blue vein under her forehead twitches just so. "But in New York I want to do something interesting. I don't want to just be a regular model. I want to be avant-garde, I'm Russian, after all."

I can't decide whether to slap her or kiss her. But I'm so drunk from all that vodka that I just keep talking. There's so many things I want to tell her all of a sudden. "Learn to think for yourself," I say. "In Moscow we're all fucked up, reacting against the past instead of evaluating the present. We've been so starved we want everything at once—to be grand, to be great. New York people are different, they take pleasure in the little quirks, the strange eccentricities." This time, perhaps it's the train, she tries hard to understand me. Furrows her brow and sits back, puts a finger against her lips as I speak. I'm penetrating her, I realize, I might be able to love her again, love her still, when she gives up. Sighs, looks out the window, pushes back from me.

"I don't always understand you," she says curtly. "Maybe after I live there for a while I'll be different." She's so gorgeous when she rejects me, her mouth a tight circle of inner affirmation. I want to kiss her, force my tongue past her unwilling lips. She goes all frigid when she's sour at me, shies away from my embraces. It turns me on though, and she knows that, backing away with a repressed smile when I move on her. When my lips brush against hers though, there's an impatient knocking on the door.

"Who's that?" she asks, alarmed.

"The conductor perhaps." I walk over and turn the oblong metal knob around, pulling back the steel door. Yeltsin stumbles in, dead drunk. Sightless, he raises a shot of vodka in the air. "Za Yeltsina," he shouts hoarsely and then falls flat on his face.

The truth is that I wasn't hip in Saratov. I sense it as soon as we embark from the train, the platform wet and slippery. I almost lose my balance when my loafers slide against the ground, fall against Irina's mother, Lyuba Fyodorovna Dmitrieva. She helps me up, crinkles her nose in that funny way Irina has sometimes. With Irina it's pretty, disarming, but on her mother it's nasty, makes her seem bitter and angry. Right away, she seems to decide I'm not serious. "What do you do, young man?" she asks me on the taxi ride home; and when I attempt to explain the business of promoting parties, the psychology of the New Russians, she switches off. Stares out the window, fans her face with an old copy of Pravda. "Things are different here. We must work for our living." She gives me a meaningful look.

Ira doesn't help at all. In Moscow, she at least pretended to sympathize with my ambitions. But here she reverts back to the dutiful provincial girl, molding her face to hide that big-city arrogance; she suppresses her Moscow habits, the naughty way she has of flexing her hips when she walks, winking at someone for the fun of it. With her mother and friends, most of them the ugly ducklings who stayed behind, she's bourgeois. Shows them pictures of our expensive apartment, wears cheap purple lipstick, drinks cup after cup of black tea. Even covers her head and buys beeswax candles when she goes to the local church. The hypocrite. Why did I ever like her? When I'm walking by the Volga river one afternoon—the local girls making eyes at me, their faces fleshy like peasants—I realize it's because she was more sophisticated than the others, a bit more cynical, had some artistic ambitions.

Here, though, she hides that side of herself, while I mope around the city. There's no space for me here in this damp, made-to-order provincial city, like so many others across Russia, which have been left to rot after the Soviet Union's collapse. The hawkers selling privatization vouchers outside the crumbling Ballet and Opera House, where the Kirov once performed, don't even attempt to hustle me, thinking me a stupid tourist. There isn't any irony anywhere, not on the shabby Lenin Avenue—its decrepit shops labeled "Bread," "Products," "Restoran," just like the Soviet times—and on the pedestrian Prospekt Kirov, with its dark kiosks selling bootleg Rasputin vodka and cafes blasting techno music, the Caucasians in their track suits leering at me as though I'm a homosexual.

It's a shock to be back. I had nurtured this romanticism of the provinces, fuelled by late-night coke sessions where someone would throw out their arms and exclaim, "Province, that's the real Russia. Birches and matryoshkas." High on the devil's dandruff I'd declaim about the stoic Volga bargemen, braving the currents in their wood-and-aluminum convoys, singing songs of lament and love in spring. The innocent, dimple-eyed provincial girls with Pushkin tucked under their arms. My mother's hippie friends, smoking bidis and staring at tea leaves, planning trips to the country, where they'd meditate near a cairn somewhere. I'd gild the few memories I had of the place before I escaped to Moscow.

But it's nothing like that at all. These days, everyone's depressed, or seems so. Their apartments are crumbling, their televisions still Nivas or Arcas, with heavy knobs for changing channels and diodes which take forever to heat up, crackling and hissing like old vinyl. The mafia's everywhere, murdering with impunity. The mother of a friend of Irina's was killed after she rejected a mobster's advances. The Mayor's office and the office of the Director of Volga Transport have new glass-and-steel facades, but otherwise nothing has changed since they erected that bridge in 1954. It was a big event, I was told. Now its pedestrian lanes are flooded with slush so thick it's difficult to walk across.

But Lyuba Fyodorovna Dmitrieva, Irina's mother, does so every morning on her way to the market, where she sells vegetables from her dacha or haggles over a tin of vegetable oil. She's not depressed—or doesn't seem so at least. "We must survive," she repeats solemnly when there's bad news on television. "We must survive." She's very busy doing so, waking up at six to walk to the market, teaching school all day, then cooking, cleaning, doing odd errands: stitching up a neighbour's jacket for a jar of pickled mushrooms. She's taken an instant dislike to me, of course. I don't help with the shopping or fix her broken stereo or even drop names as Irina does. I just take long walks along the embankment, taking pictures with the Lomo camera I've bought, or persuade Irina to ride the dinky barges down the river, guzzling vodka with the sunburnt veterans on board, who are waxing nostalgic about the old days. "They're all criminals," she'd say, "smuggling caviar and god knows what else."

So one night I head to the nightclub Chicago, the one bright-lit place in the city, and gamble for a while. Get drunk with the local mobsters, who still shave their heads and wear last year's Versace. At the blackjack table, a man in a black Prada turtleneck, his Rolex watch set to Moscow time, asks me casually whether I party at the Jazz Kafe in Moscow. When I ask him whether he knows Salminsky, he just smiles slyly. Later he goes and sits with a wiry man in a blue denim jacket who someone whispers is De Gaulle's grandson. "He's a great friend of the governor's."

Tiring of the local mobsters' company, I go over to the Frenchman's table after a while. I'm high, quite drunk, feels like another night in Moscow. They're sitting there with two pretty girls in lycra hot pants and tight stretch T-shirts; one of them with glitter on her cheeks can't be more than sixteen. When I approach, the Frenchman gets nervous, turns to the turtlenecked man and rattles off something in French. I should be more wary, but I'm used to Moscow, accustomed to playing the host.

"De Gaulle's grandson," I say in English, pulling up a chair, settling between them. "That's just great. I'm a great admirer. We Russians, unlike the Americans, have always thought well of him."

"Que voulez-vous?" he asks in French.

I wave a hand in the air, shake my head. "Oh, nothing. I'm from Moscow, know lots of people there. Just thought I'd come over and have a chat."

The Prada man leans over and hisses in my ear. "Get out. Get out. Do you understand?"

"Fuck you," I growl in an undertone. "I know lots of people in Moscow," I say, rattling off a list of names. "I'm just being friendly, you should be glad." One of the whores beckons to someone with her long-nailed fingers, glares at me, but I ignore her also.

"So," I say, raising a glass, "to Russo-French friendship." The Frenchman blows smoke in my face, scowls at me. "You're not being very friendly," I say, when I feel heavy hands push into my armpits. Before I can react, I'm lifted up into the air, dragged half-way across the club, past the entrance door, and dumped on the street. Someone bends over me, smacks me hard on the face, kicks me in the ribs, and then retreats, swearing in the choicest Russian. "You come back and we'll castrate you in the toilets."

When I stumble back to the apartment at six in the morning, Irina's in hysterics. She comes running to the door in her dressing gown when I ring the bell. "I thought you left and went back to Moscow. I'm so glad you came. I love you so much, Godunev," she cries, holding me in her arms. "Oh, no, what happened? You're bleeding all over, your lip is cut." She helps me to the kitchen, dresses my wound, is so tender, kissing my face all the while. "You'll be OK. Did you go to Chicago? That's a bad place, not like Moscow nightclubs." Later I take her to the living room and fuck her on her mother's favorite rug, the one her father brought back from Afghanistan. She tries hard not to cry out, but I thrust so hard and fast, she whimpered despite herself. It's the first time we've had sex in ages, almost a month. Back in her room, she wraps herself around me. "Forgive me," she says. "I know I haven't been there for you. I'm going to America soon, I have to think of my mother first. I might not see her for a long time." I just turn away and shut my eyes. My face hurts so much that I lie there for a while, thinking it's over between us.

In the morning, her mother's more solicitous. I don't realize it until she asks me sweetly whether I'd like milk with my coffee. "Black, of course," I answer, and she smiles warmly. Women: they like it when men are helpless, at their mercy, it brings out their mothering instinct. "Don't worry," she says, when she brings the coffee, "it's just a scratch. You were lucky, it could have been much worse."

Later she brings some photo albums and sits with me, showing pictures from her youth. I don't want to be coddled like this but am too weak to resist. "Things are so different now than they used to be. Back in our day, if a man wasn't part of the Komsomol and with a steady job somewhere, no-one trusted him. But things are different these days. Those with jobs don't get paid for months, and other, cleverer ones make the money.

"That's me," she says, pointing at a picture of a young woman with a prim scarf around her head, sipping tea at some meeting, a Komsomol one perhaps. There's another one of her on a motorcycle, a Java, wearing a leather helmet with extensions which come together under the chin. She looks glamorous, a bit of a rebel even, golden locks peeking out from under the leather cap, her chin upright. There's one of her in the Crimea, voluptuous in a beige one-piece strapless swimsuit, sharing a joke with someone outside the picture. She was quite a beauty, I realize, blond, bronzed, a Marilyn Monroe type.

"Lyuba Fyodorovna," I say, "you must have had a lot of admirers back in the day."

She blushes, wipes her lined hands against her apron.

"You know how it was then. Men wanted a girl who was serious, not just beautiful. Someone who could help build Communism."

I suppress a giggle. "Was it really like that?"

Her face darkens. "Of course!" She turns back to the stove. "At least for us it was."

It's nice being an invalid, but I can't stand it for long. It hurts my vanity, to lie there, an ice-pack around my face, while they fuss over me. It just reminds me of my folly, my silly Moscow arrogance, which doesn't mean much here in the provinces. So the next day, when they've gone shopping, I write a note and decamp from the apartment. I've decided to fly back to Moscow, visit my mother on the other side of town on the way to the airport. I've been putting it off all this while, anxious about the meeting. We haven't seen each other in years - not since my stepfather shot himself when funds for his institute dried up. I'm not sure how she's going to react. She'll be alone or with one of her arty boyfriends. So many lovers.

When I ring the bell, she doesn't open the door. I can feel her peering through the peephole, fingering the latch on the door. "Who's there?"

"It's me, Godunev. Vlad," I add, after a while. But she still doesn't open.

"Vlad's in Moscow. Who are you?"

"Tin-tin," I say at last. "Your Tin-tin. I was just passing through. Thought I'd stop by."

She hugs me when she opens the door at last; she's surprised I can tell, a bit shocked. "What's happened to you?" she asks.

"Got beat up again, Tin-tin?."

She's gotten older, more shrunken; her hair is still hennaed red, however, her small white hands heavy with rings, the apartment smelling of incense as before. The eyes are also still firm, a bit wild as they were, that touch of the soothsayer.

We sit in her cramped kitchen beneath a poster of the Indian guru Satya Sai Baba – that's new – with his frizzy Afro hair, and chat quietly. I tell her about America, about returning to Moscow, getting involved in the party scene, about my relationship with Irina, and Salminsky. She's distracted, though, "Your eyes," she says at last. "They're different. They don't see anymore like your stepfather's, just evaluating, calculating." And then we hugged and parted.

When Irina returns from Saratov, it's not the same between us. Even she realizes that, and is considering breaking off the relationship before she leaves. I'm shocked by the magnitude of my rage against her, and by my irrational feelings of anger. I hate her, I reason, for having trapped me with the money we stole from Salminsky, bound me to them in a pact from which I can't escape. I blame her for what I have become, for turning into one of them, incapable of seeing anymore? Or is it just possible that I'm in love with her, dismayed that it's so easy for her to leave her present life behind.

minus nine

Salminsky has lost his roof. It's a hot brutal summer: steam rising off the ring road; white, sperm-like balls of pukh from the poplar trees clustered on the pavements; the city so quiet you can race down the Arbat without braking. Everyone's somewhere else, in the dachas, at the Crimea, or in San Tropez, blowing their cash on ridiculous little bottles of Dom Perignon and freaking out on the staid French with their monstrous energy. But Salminsky is running around town in a black Hugo Boss suit, a Hermes scarf round his neck, plotting the Kremlin privatization and the visit of Zara Wonder. When knackered, he wipes the sweat off his face with his chubby hands and shakes them in the hot air until they're dry.

"Stop it," I plead with him. "It's over. The whole country is going to come crashing down. They're talking about a defolt, and then a rouble devaluation. The banks are going to crash, Yeltsin's going to go down. This isn't the time to go for the Kremlin. Let's wait till after the crash and see what happens."

But he doesn't believe in the crash. "It won't happen," he repeats, his eyes wild, that murderous sheen on his face. "The IMF will bail us out, the World Bank will come. All those dollars stuffed under mattresses will appear on the streets soon. It's all rumor-mongering. I'm a mathematician, I should know. Go to Fellacio and start organizing things. She's arriving in two weeks."

I should stick my tongue out and kiss him on the ear, bite off one of those hairs sticking out it, and then disappear. Catch the first flight to the south of France, get drunk with the Bykov brothers, fondle some Red Star models partying there. Start an argument with some café philosopher from Paris, tell him existentialism is just a French excuse for failure. But that's not what I do. I give Fellacio a call instead and arrange to meet him at his apartment. I want Hollywood to understand that we aren't awed by their celebrities—we can abuse them with impunity. We are Russians after all. We can destroy the entire Western world if we so desire. Call it, if you like, the last vestigial remnant of the superpower sickness.

I don't tell Joe any of this. Not that he'd mind, he'd find it titillating I'm sure. But he's not part of the inner circle: he's just a tool we're forced to use. He's got some magic with the stars, get them laid with the mobster molls. Brings Norris down to Moscow. . Has long chats with Seagal. Even succeeded in wangling an audience with Clinton when he was here for a summit. I wouldn't mind the guy—I even dig his puerile humor—if he hadn't tried to go behind my back and offer to organize the parties himself. "My girls will fuck everyone there," he had told Salminsky. "There's not going to be any horny guys heading to Dolls after." Didn't he understand that it wasn't about just getting laid, it was about creating a vibe? That was the problem with Americans: they hadn't developed in the past five years, while we had matured so fast we didn't need them any more. The times when a Sports Bar with pool tables, pinball machines, and waitresses in bobby sox was enough to draw in the crowds were over. Over.

I want to tell him all this when I stride into his apartment, but he cuts me short. He's reclining on his ottoman with some teenage girl, running his hand down her thigh, her leg stretched out in the air. "Don't worry about her," he says immediately, "she doesn't understand English." Then he tells me a joke about a woman who goes to her doctor because she wants larger breasts. "'Take a roll of toilet paper and rub it between them every morning. Come back in a month and tell me what happened,' the doctor says. 'But doctor,' she asks, incredulous, 'why would that work?' He shoots back, 'It worked with your ass, didn't it?'" I laugh despite myself. The tension's diffused momentarily, but he's still wary, I can tell. He doesn't mistake me for the Mexican Ambassador's assistant any more. We've tangled too often in the past two years for that.

"Salminsky sent you over," he says at last, while the girl runs her bright purple nails along his bald head. "He's got some plan up his sleeve. That fellow's always got something spinning around up there. If he were in Hollywood, he'd be a producer by now. All the starlets would be ambushing his mansion to get into bed with him." He pauses again, looks me over quickly. "You're growing your hair out, I see. Gives you a more casual look. I'd go with that.

"What's it about this time? That girl Sveta I sent over the other week." He throws his arms in the air. "I didn't know she had her period. You know these girls, they don't say a word because they don't want to speak English. And then, once they're there, they spoil the whole thing." He turns to his lovely. "She's not like that. When she is on the rag she goes back to her mother in Tula. Isn't that true, Lyuba?" He ruffles her hair. She isn't as cute as that one in the Starlite Diner, but still I'd go for a quick shag.

"It's not about that at all." I clear my throat. "It's a bit more serious. It's about Zara Wonder."

"Zara 'Vice City' Wonder. I'll tell you, I knew her—was it ten years ago—when she had a bit role in Police Chase 2. She was just another struggling actress then, called me once to beg an invitation for a party I was throwing." His bright eyes dance about the room, rest on a framed picture of him with his arms around Bill Clinton, and then come rushing back to me. "That's Hollywood for you, you're either small fry or a big whale. There's nothing in between." He pauses theatrically before continuing. "Just the Midwest."

He spreads his palms outwards. "Well, Godunev, I'm not invited." Shucks his eyes; lowers his voice and leans forward conspiratorial. "I think Vogue wants to keep me out of this. They want it to be a clean affair, no wild parties like when the men come visiting. Just march her through the routine and get her out safe. She's a real diva, I hear, has a violent temper.

"You'll have to go straight to Vogue. Call their Paris office, tell them you're doing a big profile on her for a top Russian magazine, want full access."

I drum my fingers against my lap. "We were going to offer you something in return."

"Me?" He punches his collarbone with his finger rapidly. He's wearing a McLenin T-shirt under his sports jacket. "What could you offer me?"

"A Lithuanian passport."

"A what? A Lithwyeenian passport. What the hell is that?"

"It's an independent nation in the Baltics. Full visa access to all European nations." I wink at him. "We thought you might use it if Uncle Sam ever decided to extradite you. We know about the mail fraud, the rape charges pending."

He colors, slaps himself on the cheeks. "That's not true, none of it. Those bitches just fabricated the story, because their Jewish lawyer thought I was an easy target. And the mail fraud is taken care of, it was a mistake. They confused me with someone else."

I raise a hand in the air. "I don't want to hear this Joe. Do you want the passport or not?"

He looks at the girl, runs his hand down her thigh again. "What do you think, Lyuba? You wanna go live in Lithwyeenia. What's the capital? Riga or something like that ainnit?"

"Vilnius."

"That's right." He furrows his brows. He seems ridiculous when he's tries to be intelligent. "That's where they had some demonstrations didn't they, in the early 90s. The TV tower, wasn't it."

"Do you want it or not?"

"I'll take it," he says quick. "How soon can you do it?"

"Within a month. We'll need some passport photos of course."

"But how about Zara Wonder?"

He rubs his hands together. "I love a challenge. I think I know her publicist, Linda, used to date a buddy of mine. We'll arrange something."

"I want to tag along with her, and we want her full itinerary."

"Jees, what you guys planning? To kidnap her?" His tongue lolls against his lower lip, he seems to be adding numbers up in his head.

"She's not worth it," he says at last. "Go for one of the men. Chuck will do whatever it is for a cut. We'll arrange the whole thing, get the media involved."

I rise. "I'll call you tomorrow to see how things are going."

Just as I'm about to leave, the doorbell rings. Joe hollers down the corridor. "Just come in, the door's open."

It's Kirk, the same as ever, pants loose around his waist, some rumpled T-shirt flapping out of his jeans, a baseball cap worn backwards. He seems embarrassed to see me here, averts his gaze, stares down at the hardwood floor. "Hey Godunev," he says, hands slack at his sides. "Surprise to see you here."

I'm feeling great now that the business has been completed. I clap him hard on the shoulders. "Yo Kirk, how's my writer doing? You keeping busy during the slow summer?" I lean forward and whisper in his ear. "Thanks for that article. Still with Masha by the way?"

He nods and then looks over at Joe. "Thanks for that," he mumbles. "She's wonderful. Great cook too."

Joe pats the couch. "Come here, Kirk. Lyuba's been waiting for you for her English lessons. Teach her some slang today, real American stuff." He shuffles towards them, gives me a backward glance before he sits down. I give them both a flamboyant wave and scoot out of there. Got some time to head to the nudist beach at Serebryanny Bor at least. Davai.

The first dinner just after she arrives is set for Shinok, Andrei Delos' Ukrainian theme restaurant with its enclosed live animal farm, a horse, some chickens, and even an old babushka knitting among them. Vogue must have thought its rustic interior and authentic Slavic menu would appeal to her sensibilities. And so it seems it does. "I just love borscht," she says as soon as she enters the private room reserved for us. "My masseur, he was Ukrainian or something like that, just made the best borscht from fresh beets and parsley." Delos appears at her side, gliding his arm around her smoothly as he helps her into their floral-patterned wooden chairs. "We use bayleaf instead of parsley, and even a bit of salo or pork fat for that authentic taste. You must try ours, made with native ingredients, and tell us what you think." He sniffs his nose in the air. "Our American guests tell us that vegetables there don't have the same taste as here. All those chemicals they add." She turns to him, shuts her eyes for a second, and then opens them again. "Most of mine are flown in fresh from Japan."

It's been a stressful week, so bad that my hands tremble when I lift the tea cup to my lips. This Kremlin thing is going to be Salminsky's Borodino. With the debts mounting up and the economy in danger of collapsing, they raised the price at the last minute, to thirty million dollars. (Logically, the cost should have come down, but this is Russia after all. They get greedier when they're being squeezed.) He's been tearing around in search of additional financing, calling moguls on their yachts, beseeching them to join him in his crazy scheme. He just didn't have that much cash available without bringing in Berezhovsky, which he's dead set against. So he ropes the Richard Gere American in at the last minute, he has some fund, Churchhouse I think, and convinces them to throw a few millions in the pot. Peter Gellen, that's his name. So coked up most of the time he doesn't see the writing on the wall. It's all going to collapse, but he's oblivious. Salminsky took him to Luzhniki, that private dacha enclave, got him some Red Star models, gave him the five star mafioso treatment, and he signed his firm's name on the dotted line. The fool. Well, at least our dollars are still safe. At one point, high on coke, he grabbed me around the neck, and begged that I contribute. "It's just a half a million," I cried. "What difference does it make? I need something to fall back upon if all this goes to the dogs." Then that wolf Kirsanov changed his mind at some point when he heard she was forty years old. "She's a babushka," he bellowed. "I don't want no babushka. Get me someone fresher, younger, Cindy Crawford perhaps." But after he sounded out his buddies he came back. "She'll do."

So here we are. Apart from me and Joe, there's that egomaniac filmmaker Nikita Mikhailkov with his Prussian mustache; some suit from Paris Vogue, fat slob, carnation bowtie, hair swooped over his bald spot. Then there's the matronly editor-in-chief of Russian Vogue, a former television producer, Wonder's publicist, Joe's old pal, her young stylist; and four bodyguards, all identical, like lifeguards from Baywatch, microphones attached to their lapels. They're sitting at a side table, whispering quiet among themselves. One's stationed at the entrance to the room, running a nervous hand down his shoulder-length blond hair.

Zara Wonder's not quite glamorous, not in the sense that we Russians conceive of the term: ultra-sexy, and arrogant as an apparatchik. She's really nothing like she is in the movies; with her blond hair tied back in a ponytail, and her breasts hidden under a single-breasted champagne-colored suit, she might be another aging model at the Jazz Kafe. Granted, there's a charm to her lustrous lips and shimmering white teeth; her skin glistens too, from all the lotions she must use. And her Bulgari necklace is, well, a genuine Bulgari. But it's her expression that intimidates even Godunev—it's so focused, so attuned to everything going on around her, that we're all a bit jittery and fearful of uttering the wrong phrase or word. I've been around so many bimbos, I've forgotten what mature women are like. She's just gotten married, we know, so there's a radiance about her, an inner happiness that shows through immediately.

Mikhailkov is the first to take the plunge. He's met her before at the Oscars, and elsewhere among the glitterati.

"So what are you working on these days? I've heard rumors there's going to be a sequel to Vice City. Is that true?"

She turns her head to the side and laughs, self-conscious. It's a wonderful laugh, not quite sincere, but still melodious—cut off abruptly just when you want more. "That's being going around for years. I'm not even sure I'd want to act in a sequel: I've graduated from blond seductress roles, I think."

He nods his head gravely, raises his eyebrows. "So you are doing something else, then?"

"Oh, let me think. Well, I'm lending my voice to Spiderz. It's a relief to be reduced to just a voice, a sonic presence, and not have to think about your body."

"Spiders! Is that an animated feature?"

She laughs again, a quick one, closer to a chortle. "Yes, it's a love story. Quite charming in fact, if you're an arachnophile. I always was. Never scared of them, even as a child." Her voice is American, it's a bit of a surprise, but there's a monotonous aspect to her speech, a deeper undertone, which makes her sound Continental. Not as Yankish as Joe or Kirk.

"Yes, animation films are quite popular these days. There's a Czech director who makes wonderful animated films about Alice in Wonderland and Kafka. But we Russians stick closer to the grain."

She smiles generously again, those teeth of hers. "I'm fascinated by this place." Looks around and raises her eyebrows. Her eyes are blue, I notice, but the pupils are dark, mysterious. That's what gives her the seductress look, those gypsy pupils trapped inside the blue iris.

"Things have changed so much in the last ten years. I remember when it was the 'Evil Empire,'" she says, booming out the phrase. "My father fought in the war, was in Germany somewhere. And then of course there's the artists, Stanislavsky, Nijinsky, Nureyev. Am I pronouncing them right?"

"Yes, yes, of course."

It's my turn to take the cue. "Don't forget our writers. Dostoevsky, Tolstoy, Pushkin and Lermentov. Lermentov is my favorite, though. He's a true romantic, a Russian Oscar Wilde."

"Really? I never heard of him. Is he translated?"

"I think so. He's not part of the canon like some of the others. But I'll try to find you a copy here."

"I'd love that. You know I was a bookworm as a child. Just read all the time, didn't do much else. The name of my production company Quark comes from James Joyce." She shakes her head. "Although the gossip columnists don't think so, of course."

After that, it's as easy as blini and caviar. I take Joe's advice and praise her role in Paul Tyson's 'Goodbye Evenings'. "I always wondered who that pretty girl on the bike was until I discovered quite recently it was you," I say. She likes that, even blushes a little. "I'm so surprised you remember that role. That was my first break. Oh God, how good it felt then. Just even to be a face in a film. To work with an acclaimed director after doing so much drivel for television."

Joe then says some kind words about her recent appearance on

Leno, and about her strong performance as Violet in Paul Tyson's Oscar-winning Red Hoppers, and we we're in like Flynn. Or as Russians say, we snared the bear. The rest is Delos' work. She loves the borscht. "It's almost spicy. I didn't realize it could be so aromatic." We force her to try a cottage-cheese-stuffed vareniki and she goes yum. Then I explain the mafia to her, say there wasn't so much of a mob as biznismen acting in their own interests. They're quite legitimate, wear suits and all, even speak English, some have studied in the West. It's just that they take the law into their own hands sometimes.

She puts the napkin on the table and gives another one of her movie star smiles. "That makes me feel so much better. I had this fear of the mafia, that they might try to kidnap me or do something horrible. Or I'd be caught in a shoot-out. But it seems quite peaceful here. I loved the drive in from the airport, the time we passed the Kremlin for the first time, those spires gleaming in the night."

When she's leaving, she presses my hand polite. "What was your name again?"

"Godunev, Miss Wonder."

She laughs again, so carefree. This is what it must be like when you're rich and famous. "Just call me Zara. That's fine." Then she pats me quickly on the head. "I hope I'll see you tomorrow. At the launch party at least."

"Oh, I'll come with you to the Pushkin in the afternoon. It's my favorite museum."

Afterwards, Joe comes and puts his arm around me. "Godunev, well done. You could charm a sledgehammer, I'm sure."

Then he leans closer. "You're not planning to kidnap her or do something mad, are you? I don't want to get into trouble."

I run a hand along his bald head. "Don't chatter your teeth for no reason. We just want to make new friends."

Catching him buffing his loafers in the restroom under one of those shoe polish machines that are popping up everywhere, I squeeze his shoulder. "Don't worry, no-one's going to get killed." He holds his foot out and admires his shoe proudly. "I just bought a new pair, don't want to get them bloody yet."

That's my idea, I want to tell him, but I don't. I'm not as vicious as some of the others might think. Just so you know, I refused to 'lend my tongue' unless the sacrificial kids were taken from the morgue, not from the streets. "Why kill street urchins when we can get perfectly preserved dead ones? No-one will know the difference anyway." I love kids, I told them, especially the ones out there on the streets, the orphans, making do for themselves. I can't be that cruel. They had agreed, reluctantly, looked at me a bit askance. The pressure was even greater now that concessions had been made; I had the sense that I would not be pardoned if I fucked up this time.

She wears an emerald green Givenchy gown to the Pushkin Museum, her blond hair loose, covering her pert ears with their curly bangs. Gliding up the carpeted stairs in her pink Bruno Magli stilettos, the ruffled edges of her lustrous dress almost grazing the floor, she looks positively glamorous. Like a movie star at last. A murmur goes through the crowd trailing her when she stops besides a Donatello masterpiece, reaches her hand out, almost touching it. She's worn gloves for the occasion, cream gloves, soft as sour cream. Her entourage is jerked into motion again when she waves her head and moves on, striding fast past the Florentine masterpieces, and into the Impressionist room with its high ribbed ceiling and impressive collection of Matisse, Picasso, Renoir, Bonnard, and others. The Director of the Museum, nervous in a shiny, polyester suit, tape holding the neck of his glasses together, hangs on her every word, elaborating on the works in his bookish English. "These paintings here came from the collections of the Morozovs, who were famous merchants before the revolution…"

I hang back, fuming, at the edge of the throng, half expecting she'll turn back and beckon me to her side. But there's none of the familiar intimacy of last night. When entering she gave me the briefest of nods as I stood with Joe near the ticket office, and then moved past us to waltz up the stairway, her publicist half-running to catch up with her. "These old ladies," I heard her declaim, "they're just so charming. I wonder at all the things they've seen in their lifetimes." The museum has been closed off for her visit and that infuriates me even more. Long lines snake around the corner of the museum, families from the provinces sweating in the summer heat outside, too poor to slake their thirst with a Pepsi or Coke from the kiosks near the metro. The damn bitch, I think. Not even a wave for the crowds, a gesture to compensate them for their long wait. Instead she had demanded that her Zil stretch limousine—once used by the Politburo—drive up right to the entrance, into the garden itself, so she didn't have to risk a run-in with the masses.

I want to have her brought down to earth, among the fallen ones. The Gibertis and Donatellos hold no appeal this afternoon, neither do Picasso's paintings from his Blue period, nor do the feverish Bonnards, the colors so intense and suffused they once made me swoon. There was a time when I'd come here and lose myself, wandering from painting to painting, meditating on the brush strokes. I thought I detected in Gauguin's erotic nudes some hidden code, a message passed through the sands of time. Were the pink of the sand and the violet of the Tahitian girl's blouse intentional? We Russians never quite understood Impressionism, we stumbled upon it a century later, when it was old hat in France. Even Dobryshinsky's early pastorals in that style are too crude, too dark. They have none of the lightness of the Impressionists with their keen sense of color and sensuality. There's an energy which races through their works, of absinthe, dog-day afternoons, hazy and hot, a brook babbling in the distance somewhere. Even our Chagall seems clumsy, a trickster, daubing in exotic Russian images to please the Parisian gentry.

But that's not what goes through my mind this afternoon. I remember that I once wanted to enter these paintings, to become them. I imagined that there'd be a time when I'd experience the pleasure of lazing with a picnic basket of cheese and wine in a wooded glade somewhere in the south, where the bright sun was a presence so strong it imbued my senses with an unbearable lightness of being. I was stoned sometimes, yes, but that wasn't important. I'd leave the Pushkin and wander down to the embankment, poke a delicate foot into the Moscow River if it was spring or summer and then yank it out, kick it in the air carefree. But this time I can't focus on the works, their symbolism remains hidden from my senses. I see canvases and paint and bursts of color. But that's it. My mind is elsewhere, on our dollars deposited in Riga. On tonight's launch party and the preparations for later. The phone keeps ringing. Either it's Salminsky or the men we've hired to carry out the task later that evening.

At some point, I peel my eyes from the glass casing of a Picasso. They're strange, the pupils contracted into expressionless points. Have I lost the power to see?

Zara Wonder certainly has. She barely pauses before a single canvas, gives a nod at the Picassos, and then strides on quickly through the other rooms. She's done this a hundred times before, I presume, visited museums out of a sense of obligation to her hosts, and it doesn't mean a thing. Within an hour she's through, rushing out with her entourage, quick into the black Zil, zipping back to the hotel. "She wants to call her husband and rest up before tonight," whispers Linda. "She's still jet-lagged even though she stopped at London on the way over."

I stumble out of there as if I am drugged. It's so hot and humid I break out into sweat, despite the summery light linen slacks and ribbed cotton T-shirt. The crowd presses against the gate, restless, the babies still wrapped in blankets and jerseys as if it were winter. Russian mothers!

On an impulse I walk to the nearest kiosk and purchase four litres of chilled Coca Cola. Walking back, I hand them out at random to some of the people in the line. "Drink," I exhort. "Drink and slake your thirst."

"Vodka," offers an impish youth in a pair of fake Levis. "Why waste Coke without mixing it with vodka?" So I have a swig with him and then hail a taxi back to the apartment. So much work remains to be done.

The glitzy bash for the launch of Russian Vogue at the Radisson Slavyanskaya Hotel evokes the scene on the deck of the Titanic just minutes after it hit the iceberg. I didn't come up with the cliché: it's on the tongues of Moscow's wags the past few weeks every time there's a glamorous fiesta. This time the Richard Gere lookalike sidles up to me as everyone mingles stiffly in the foyer of the American Theater, glomming onto the waiters as they pass with their silver trays heavy with fluted champagne glasses. Gulp, gulp, go the guests, their determined eyes tracking the champagne waiters. There's a desperate desire to get drunk as fast as possible. Even Godunev is swept up in the general hysteria, downing glass after glass, until his cheeks are flushed, a little vein under the forehead going tic-toc. So peaceful again!

"Just like the Titanic, isn't it?" he says. "Everyone's running scared." The Gere look-alike is wearing a smart tux tonight, his hair gelled and swept to the side of his head in a Beach Boys pomade; he's washed his face in Clinique lotion this evening, it glistens just as Zara Wonder's does.

I spill some Veuve Cliquot on the sleeve of his jacket out of spite. "I've heard that line a hundred times before. Did you just come up with it?"

"No, seriously," he says, a tad offended. "Look around, they're all pretending to have fun, but they're scared shitless they'll lose their shirts."

"And what about you? Your fund managers aren't pulling their hairs out?"

He smiles, does that famous shrug of his. "Oh, we're tied up in oil and gas. Solid investments." He winks. "And some proposed art acquisitions. A rouble devaluation is just a ripple in our portfolio.

"How's Irina?" he asks, changing the subject. "I hear she's having quite a fabulous time in New York, Jack Nicholson coming to her birthday party at Spy Bar."

"How do you know?"

He twirls his hand in the air. "The grapevine, heard it at some party."

I tap him gently on the shoulder. "I might have a surprise for you later in the evening. Stick close." Then I push through the crowd, searching out familiar faces. The tusovka—at least the ones not in the South of France—are out in force tonight. Bartenev struts about in his psychedelic T-shirt and Mickey Mouse hat, Masha Tsigal is there, hugging someone as usual. Mikhailkov stands in the center near the staircase and waits for guests to come up and shake his hand. The oligarch Gusinsky from NTV is there; so is Yeltsin's press secretary. A few black-clad Americans in cocktail dresses scurry around, shooing everyone into the auditorium. A Molotov Cock model comes up to me. "I've got a multiple-entry visa to America," she whispers. "Anything happens, there's a plane waiting for us at Domodedovo airport. I suggest you talk to Sergei about getting on the list." I brush her off and accost Salminsky. He's stylish for the occasion, just a white T-shirt under a Ralph Lauren jacket, thick, black-rimmed German glasses stuck on his face for effect. He's already drunk and coked-up, grabs me around the neck as soon as I approach, and throws me in the direction of some model. "Get to know her. You're single again, enjoy yourself."

I extricate myself and lean towards him. "What about the rouble? There's a lot of whispering going on here."

He wags his finger in the air. "Nothing's going to happen. I've spoken to Kiriyenko, he's a friend of mine. And you heard what Yeltsin said yesterday."

He turns in the direction of Zara Wonder, who's pressed into a corner, flashes going off around her, and declaims loudly. "Russians are so used to crazy things happening, they will them into being. But this time they're wrong."

I can't reason with him. It's too late at this point anyway. I tag Salminsky into the auditorium. It's a fairly standard presentation: Mario Testino's shots of Kate Moss in some Sheremetyov mansion, taken specially for Russian Vogue, are flashed on the screen, and then there's a few speeches. 'Historic occasion.' 'Opening up Russia to the West.' 'Not since the Russian Revolution has Russia been so fashion-conscious as it is now. The growing middle class etc. Yak, yak.' When Zara Wonder comes on stage there's a silence. The murmuring stops and everyone gawks at her. She's gorgeous again, damn!, a violet Vera Wang skirt held together with a rhinestone button, and a bodice above of illusion netting, so fine she seems topless. A slight gasp goes through the audience. From a distance she looks so fabulous and unapproachable. She raises her hand in the air, "Spasibo," she says in Russian, to some cheers, and then gives a short speech. It's concise and surprisingly moving. "When I was a young girl growing up in Pennsylvannia, I always imagined Russia to be grey and drab, like the suburbs of Pittsburgh." A titter from the audience. "And even coming here I admit to a certain apprehension. But in the past twenty hours I've been impressed by the elegance and sophistication of the people I've met. And with the tremendous changes that have taken place here in the last seven years." She raises her eyes at the audience. "And by the beauty of your women, some of whom I've had the pleasure of meeting back in America." Loud clapping, some cheering. "I think Vogue should be privileged to be printing their magazine in a language so rich and historic as yours is. Spasibo."

Then she coos with the baby of one of the publishers for a while, rocks it in her arms (she's trying to dispel her blond seductress image, I conjecture) and exits gracefully from the stage. Later she barely stays at the reception in the conference hall. Even the large roasted pigs don't detain her. She skips through the room haughtily with her entourage, shakes a couple of hands, makes some polite chit-chat with the biggest of the big-wigs, and then heads for the door. When she leaves the banquet room with a last-minute flourish I place a call to the motorcyclists. Bark down the phone. "Rev up your bikes. She's coming." Then I call the two cops from the Arbatskaya precinct. "Keep the boys ready. Her ZiL should be passing in ten minutes. And remember," I add, my voice menacing, "don't be soft. Use those Kalashnikovs."

We've mapped out her route in advance. She's going straight back to the hotel, according to her publicist, so we figure the car will drive up the bridge, then down Zubovsky Boulevard, up the Arbat, make a turn to the right near the Kremlin, and then drive straight down to the Baltschug, where she's staying. There's going to be an after-party at the hotel later for a few select guests. Joe had cajoled her into agreeing to that after he said the photographs of World War II sold there would go to charity. To an orphanage for children with Down's Syndrome. How could she refuse? Perfect. The cops and the dead kids are waiting on the Arbat, just opposite the Sports Bar, with their nasty little surprise for her entourage.

Just as she's leaving I run up to Linda and ask her if two of us can accompany her in the car. "It's pretty unusual," she says. "We usually travel as a group."

"It's a ZiL," I say, "there's plenty of room."

She nods in assent. Running up to Gere and Joe, I ask them to join her in the car. "That'll be swell," says Gere, puffing up. "How do you manage things like that?"

Joe senses a rat. "Are you sure?" he asks. "I've got my driver waiting for me outside."

"Just go," I tell him. "She wants some company on the way back."

About fifteen minutes after they've left, I head downstairs and hail

Salminsky's Mercedes. "Payecchali. To the Arbat." Just before I leave though, I bump into Kirk in the lobby. He looks smart for once, well, stylish for a journalist. A white shirt under a sports jacket, even some scroungy tie for the effect. "I'm writing this up for the Moscow Times," he says, smiling, his arm around Masha. "Great party, isn't it?" He gestures with his thumb towards the downstairs restroom. "Mark from the eXile is here. The rumour is he's overdosed on some ketamine and is hiding in the toilet. He's sweating as much as a Sumo wrestler. Do you have some coke to perk him up?"

I pat him on the cheek affectionately. "Here, take some to him. You Yanks can't handle your drugs." I bend closer and whisper in his ear. "Don't file your story yet. Wait a bit. There might be a big scoop."

"Yeah, what?"

I smile mysteriously. "You'll see. Just watch the wires when you get back."

Then I give him the high five and hurry out of there. Stupid, I think now. So stupid. So I snort a quick line of coke from another bag in the back of the car, until I realize there's no sense in admonishing myself any longer. I just want to dance.

As we're driving up the bridge, the Camel sign flashing high on our right, my apartment up there, I construct the scene in my mind. The motorcycles following them, the masked drivers firing shots into the air. "Faster," she must be begging the driver, "faster. What's going on?" Perhaps a shot or two skidding off the roof, just to give them a scare. Then with the driver speeding, nervous, his attention focused on the rearview mirror, the dead kids suddenly appear in front, out of the dark. Bam, dead. Would the driver attempt to run? I guess he might, but we've the GAI car stationed in front to block their path. It's unlikely that things won't go according to plan. We've coached them well.

I see the crowd as soon as we turn on the Arbat. There's sirens flashing, cars parked in the middle of the road, blocking the traffic, restless people milling about. I sight some whores, dainty in their high heels, crossing the street to check out the action. Parking the car near the Metellitsa casino, I step out and run towards them, pushing through the crowd. "GRU," I shout, "GRU," and everyone moves aside. When I get there it's just as I wanted. Zara Wonder is pushed against the hood, her hands on the roof, while one of the cops prods her with the butt of his Kalashnikov and screams invectives in Russian. Joe and Gere are also pressed up against the car, their hands handcuffed behind their backs. Linda and the bodyguards stand to the side, nervous, fidgeting with their hands.

"Passport!" screams one of the cops when I arrive. "Passport! Where's your fucking passport?"

"I left it at the hotel," whimpers the actress. "I didn't know you had to carry it with you. I don't do that in LA." Gere I notice is translating for her, his teeth clenched.

"This is Russia. We don't follow American laws, we follow Russian ones." He prods her again with the gun. "What's in that bag at your feet?"

"Nothing. Just personal stuff."

"Show me," he demands, and as she bends down to pick up the bag, she catches sight of me.

"You," she says unbelieving, "you were at the restaurant. Help me, please. These men are monsters. They're drunk too. They want to take me to the police station. It wasn't our fault believe me. Those kids just appeared out of the blue. We were being followed by some gunmen on bikes. Do something, please. Call my lawyer, his number is." She rattles off some LA number, she's so hysterical I can barely understand her. "Easy," I say soothing. "Easy! I'll try to sort this out."

"Godunev," shouts Joe, "call Salminsky. Use your power. I haven't seen GAI like this before. Are they specnaz?"

I hold up a hand. "Wait, I'll try to sort it out."

"Come here," I say to one of the cops. He pretends, as we had agreed, that he doesn't know me. "Passport," he barks. After I show him my passport, he relaxes a bit. We have a long heated talk, waving our arms about, almost at each other's throats at one point. I'm enjoying this, haven't had so much fun since those first parties. I wish this altercation could go on forever, terrified Wonder seething against the car, sweat pouring down her armpits. But the other GAI might arrive soon and things would get even more complicated. So, winking at Gere, I hand the two cops five crisp Benjamins, and come to an agreement. Everyone, except Zara Wonder, will go the police station to testify. They'll all be released later, I promise them. A friend of mine—i.e., Salminsky—will come later to make sure things are fine. A policeman will visit her later in the hotel room to take down her report. There's a collective sigh of relief. "I can't believe this shit," screams Gere. "There's a couple hundred dollars in my wallet. Take it and let me go." The cop is tempted, I can tell, but I give him a stern nod.

"Let's go," I tell the star. "I've got a car down the road from here. We'll use it. It's better." As she walks towards the car, sweaty, her hair disheveled, the crowd swells around us. Most don't recognize her as Zara Wonder—they haven't seen the television yet—they're more interested in her transparent bodice. "How much did you pay?" yells someone. "I didn't think you could find such girls on the Arbat."

A passing backpacker, goodness knows what he's doing here at this hour, recognizes her. "Zara Wonder," he screams. "It wasn't your fault." She gives him a grateful wave.

When we're safely in the car she's all mine. We've eliminated her entire entourage and there's no-one left except me. She's still hysterical, babbles about the masked motorcyclists. "What were they doing?" she keeps asking. "I can't understand why they'd be chasing our car. It reminds me of Princess Diana. It's frightening isn't it? Perhaps they meant us to crash."

"There's something going on," I say darkly. "Russia's about to default on their debt. Perhaps someone thought they'd score points with this. It's heinous, terrible." I play up the role of the hurt Russian, the naïve citizen who can't understand the machinations of his leaders. I tell her about the "Faces in the Snow" incident with Gusinsky, instigated by Korzhakov. "Not even the oligarchs know what's happening sometimes. Russia is a riddle wrapped inside an enigma." At one point she holds my hand, pats it. "Thank you," she says, her voice soft, and kisses me on the lips. "Thank you so much." She's still not lost her film star vanity, thinks she's doing me a great favor. I just blush and smile, embarrassed, pretend to be honored. Wait till tomorrow. We'll roast you on the spit.

When we get back to her room at the hotel, I offer a line of cocaine. She laughs again, a weak imitation of her former one. "I haven't done that shit in years. Not since I was a model in New York." But she's so stressed and dazed, she assents with a slight tilt of her head. I make her a thick line and watch as she snorts it up greedily. Later her eyes get focused, she shifts restlessly on the bed. Starts to blab again, wants to call her husband, her lawyer. "I hate Russia," she whines in a thin voice. "I hate this fucking country."

"Chill out," I say, and offer her some vodka. She gulps the small bottle down. "Do you have a smoke?" she asks. Blushes a bit, closes her eyes in that seductive way of hers. "I don't usually smoke except in the movies. But tonight I guess I'll make an exception."

"This is more real than the movies," she says later, puffing on the Parliament Light. "Do you have any idea what's going on?"

I pick up my mobile and stare at it as if it were an enemy. "I will soon. I hope to find out who's behind this madness. But I must go now. I have to make some calls."

When I'm leaving, she asks in a timid voice. "What about the party?"

I wave a dismissive hand. "Oh forget about it. I'll tell everyone it's cancelled. Just relax and talk to your friends. I'll be back in a few hours with some news."

Outside it's chaos, as I had expected. Policemen have cordoned off the hotel from the public. My phone rings constantly. Even some of our closest friends don't know we had anything to do with this. Most think, as we had predicted, that it's the Kremlin's doing. They want to send a message to the IMF. If you don't shell out some more billions, Russia's going to descend further into anarchy as it already is. Their chief negotiator Anatoly Chubais is in Washington at the moment talking with the Clinton administration. This might be his bargaining tool. The wags think he'll say, "Look, we're losing control already. The oligarchs are waging war against each other, they're targeting America for mandating reform and then not bailing us out. Can you imagine what'll happen if Russia collapses?" etc. etc.

Great I think. I call Salminsky to congratulate him. "All according to plan," I tell him. "No-one suspects us."

"Come to Rasputin," he says. "It's rebuilt now after the fire. We're turning our heads inside out."

Three hours later I knock at her door again. She opens it immediately after peering through the peephole. She's been watching Dynasty on television, she's changed into a silk bathrobe. She's drunk, I can tell, and still a bit on edge from the coke.

"There's a funeral service at two tomorrow afternoon. I think it'll be a good gesture if you come."

She chucks her eyes. "So soon. It all just happened a few hours ago."

"This is high profile," I tell her. "The Moscow mayor's gotten involved. Promised to seek out the masked men. He seems to think, as many others do, that Yeltsin's behind it."

Her eyes widen again. "Yeltsin? The President?"

I try to explain the situation as concisely as I can. The impending default, the IMF loan, the attempt to put pressure on the US government. "Oh my God," she says, "I'm just a pawn, a pawn in a big game. That's just what my husband said, he's a newspaper editor you know. 'Russia's full of intrigue,' he had said, 'it's got nothing to do with you. Somebody thought they could use your presence for their own purposes.' He's so smart," she says, and then breaks off, lost in thought. "Oh, I wish I could just get a plane now and fly out of here. I'm so scared. My lawyer says he can't do anything unless they do something drastic like throw me into jail."

I go up to her and give her a rose I've been hiding behind my back. "It's for you. I can't stop thinking about you." She gives me another chaste kiss on the lips. "You're so sweet. You're like …"—she thinks for a second, crinkles her brow—"like the Good Samaritan. I don't know what I'd do without you."

I stare her in the eyes. "You'll come then. I'll pick you up of course."

"My plane's at six, though."

"That gives you plenty of time. Pack your bags in the morning. I'll take you straight to the airport after the service. You can wait there for the flight if you have extra time."

She wrings her hands. "But I don't have a black dress. I wasn't planning on something like this."

"What are your measurements? I'll get you one in the morning. I'll pick it up at Versace. They have some wonderful stuff."

She comes up to me and ruffles my hair. "Thank you so much. You're an angel."

When I'm leaving, I hand her an Imovane sleeping pill. "That's for you. In case you have trouble sleeping."

She's used the Imovane. I can tell that as soon as I see her in the morning. She's refreshed, her eyes clear, almost sparkling, the movie star smile back on her face.

"Come in," she says, yawns once I enter, lifting her arms in the air languidly.

"Oh god, what time is it? I didn't sleep till late. The police came right after you left."

"How was it?"

She flashes me a coquettish look. "A piece of cake. They were almost apologetic. You had something do with it, didn't you?" For a moment I think we might be lovers, meeting at odd hours of the night when she wearies of her persona. But then she reaches for the phone to call room service and her voice is so controlled, so sprite, the old resentments return.

I plunk down on her unmade bed as I were home and surf channels on her television. "I've brought you a dress," I announce, almost as an aside. "I hope you like it." It's an ebony-black Versace gown with gold lining on its collars. The buttons were gold too but I had them replaced. There's nothing to be done about that touch of flashiness near the neck except wear a thick scarf, as I suggest. Even though its summer.

"Oh, its gorgeous," she purrs. "It's perfect for the occasion except for that …" She looks up at me, shakes her hair about. "How much was it?"

I pretend I haven't heard her. "We can breakfast downstairs if you like. They've got a wonderful brunch with Norwegian salmon and caviar."

"How much was it?" she asks again and then gives up, giving me an admonishing look, a shadow of a smile playing on her lips. Let her believe I'm in love with her, I think. It'll just make things easier.

"Let's stay here," she announces. "I'm just not ready to deal with people yet."

"How are the others?"

She pauses, then tch-tches loud. "They're fine, I think, sleeping right now. They had quite a rough time last night." I smile inside. That's what we intended. Salminsky showed up drunk at seven a.m. to bail them out. They had been dumped in the holding cell with drunks and prostitutes from Tverskaya. The drunks had wanted to beat up her faggish bodyguards, I heard. They thought they were some gay boys from Chance, hauled in for drug possession. Gere, I'm told, saved the day, making some impassioned defense in Russian. The fool! He's American, though, I reason. Probably doesn't get much of a chance to exercise his patriotic side.

So we sit there, sit by side on the bed, and gobble up her breakfast hungrily, eating the hard white rolls even, smearing them with butter and biting off chunks so that crumbs fall on the bedsheets. It's intimate, almost sensual in a weird way. Close up—and without her creams and perfumes—she's not even beautiful, though. She's short, for one, much shorter than I had imagined, a couple of inches less than Irina, and her chin and jowls are so sharply-cut, they seem a tad masculine. Her eyes, those famous seductress eyes, are fatigued; deprived of an audience they don't mock or joust as they do in public. Instead they curl up inside themselves, turn vapid—and yes, even trusting.

She gazes at me again tenderly, and I wonder whether she wants me to kiss her. So I bend forwards on the bed and rub her around the neck, entangling her mouth within mine when she drops her head. We stay like that, passionate, until a gun goes rat-a-tat on the TV, and she jumps up.

"Got to change. It'll take a while. There's some whiskey in the mini-bar if you'd like some."

There's a small crowd outside the obscure church in Yugo Zapadnaya we've chosen as the venue. Mostly hacks, journalists, the regular suspects, CNN, BBC, The New York Times, The Moscow Times etc. They shove their long-necked microphones in her face but she brushes past, her bodyguards at her side. They're here with us, knackered and glum, quiet as tombs, but doing their job. Her publicist Linda tries to be vivacious, making a joke about four weddings and a funeral, reminding her boss of the nuptials in the past month, but falls silent as we trudge through the heat to the doors of the Orthodox Church. Once we're there, I bar the entrance, my hands stretched outwards. "No-one allowed except for Zara Wonder."

She interrupts. "But my bodyguards…" Her eyes convey a silent plea, but she trusts me so much at this point she just nods assent and follows me inside when I frown and shake my head from side to side. "Wait outside," I tell them. "We won't be long. And don't talk to the media."

We've stuffed the cosy church inside with lackeys, babushkas and assorted pensioners we've bribed with a few dollars and instructed not to interfere, no matter what happens. Upstairs, on the slim balcony of the inner onion dome, are men with guns pointed at the gathering. Just in case. The two boys are placed in identical birch wood coffins near the iconostasis, a priest in a diadem and a silver-spangled gown reciting Slavic hymns over them. When we walk over to the coffins, she gasps. Crosses herself and falls to her feet. "Oh, my God! What have we done," she cries. Standing up, she places a hand across each of her breasts and recites a silent prayer for herself. I'm moved again, for just an instant, with pity for the kids. If we had cut their lives short, as the others intended, I might hate myself at this moment. The knowledge that I saved the lives of two others like them, pickpockets, skulking the Arbat hustling tourists, makes this charade bearable.

We're approaching the moment of my greatest triumph I think. What are the parties I've organized compared to this show, this theater of the absurd? But instead of gloating, getting all giddy inside, I just feel empty, devoid of emotion. Years ago I might have thrilled to the lit candelabras hanging from the ceiling, the smoky icons of the Virgin Mary and St. George slaying the dragon, the harmony of the hymnal in Old Slavonic. I would have gazed upwards at the sliver of light squeezing through the glazed windows near the roof of the dome and conjured up a poem of Tsvetaeva from memory. This time though I am tense, calculating the right moment to nudge her towards the iconostasis.

"Here," I whisper when she's done paying her respects. "This way."

"Where?" She seems confused. "Isn't the Mayor of Moscow supposed to be here?"

I whisper in her ear. "He's coming. But first we must pay our respects to their father."

"Oh yes, their father. I had forgotten."

I lead her to the broad wall of the iconostasis, open the door at its side, and cajole her inside. Once she's in the inner room, I lock the door shut behind us. She's trapped. Of course she doesn't realize it at first. Salminsky comes towards us. He's radiant, suave in a black Savile suit, a heavy Orthodox cross round his neck. "My condolences," he says, bowing with servility. "I was at the police station this morning. A most unfortunate affair." He raises his eyes towards the ceiling. "They play with us all the time here in Russia. Without concern for the common man." Shakes his head grim, extends his hand.

"Meet the father of those two children. Sergei Kirsanov."

It's him of course, the dreaded guardian of the Kremlin. He's dressed as he always is, in a baggy double-breasted pigeon-gray suit, the buttons bearing the double-headed eagle insignia of the Russian state. He's wearing a jade ring which once belonged to Ivan the Terrible on his pinkie; he waves it at her when she turns and says, "I'm sorry." She's a bit stumped, surprised I can tell that he's so well-heeled, not a sorry, old man with a cheap Cardigan, as she was expecting. But she hides her feelings well, acts gracious, bends a little when she clasps his hand. For a while, Kirsanov does nothing. He holds her hand in his for a long time, stares into her eyes, a pathetic smile plastered on his face. He might call it all off, I think, exchanging glances with Salminsky. He might, who knows. But Zara makes the mistake of gently moving to disentangle her hand from his. He grabs it tighter instead when he senses her subtle withdrawal, and pulls her towards him roughly.

Kirsanov screams in accented English, sticking his face close to her, just as we had rehearsed. "You're in the plot aren't you? How much did they pay you? A million dollars? Two million? I'll have you tortured right here before you escape." Her eyes wide, terror conquering her proud demeanor, she turns to me again. "What's going on? What plot?"

He grabs her hair. "Listen me. Those me kids. You are knowing who I am. I'm head of mafia here. Big plot, steal kids, and throw them under you car. Why?"

She tries to shout but her voice is just a whimper. "Don't pull my hair like that. Do you know who I am?"

"Yes, I know you" he shouts, slapping her fast across the face. "You Medusa, killing own children. You child killer. You die." He slaps her again, a bit softer this time. She breaks into sobs, covers her face with her hands, and screams. Howls in fact. "Help me, help me."

He comes up and muffles her. "Scream, shout," he cries, "but they not hear. They my friends. They hear they get shot. Understand."

"I didn't know, I had no idea who the father was," I insist when he releases her. "It's some big mistake."

She whimpers again. "Is he going to kill me? What does he want?"

I must admit I'm impressed, hadn't realized the brute possessed such power of intimidation. Must have learned it over at the KGB's Lubyanka headquarters.

He pushes his face close to her and spits, hitting her in the eye. "Not only you I kill but husband also. Send killer to America. An eye for an eye. *Pani mayesh. Pani mayesh Russkie*," he says, speaking fast in Russian, threatening, cajoling, spitting.

"I don't understand, no, no," she cries. "Speak English."

But he refuses, just stalks around, menacingly, screaming out invectives. The Russian language is rich in them, so rich, and Kirsanov must be the master. Job tvoi mat, durak, pashol nachyui, and on and on he goes, hurling insults I haven't heard in years.

She just stands there cowering, her face still hidden, sobbing silently, a suppressed scream at times. "Godunev," she cries, so I go over. "It's all right," I whisper. "I'm here. He'll never get away with this."

It's my turn now. I go over to him and pretend to reason with him while he stalks around the tiny room. He's so incensed though, so caught up in his part that he just keeps cursing while I gently remind him of our pact. At one point he pushes me away so roughly I fall against a stool in the corner. "Fuck you," he says in English, and then keeps pacing. His aggression seems so real I'm afraid for a bit he might renege on our plans. The brute is so unpredictable, he might just kill her for the hell of it. So that he can boast he's done the impossible. He's been known to order the killing of factory directors who didn't deign to send him an expensive gift for the New Year. "Kirsanov," I scream in Russian, losing control."

But he spits and pulls out a Makarov instead. "I'll kill you all. All of you. Russia's collapsing and you want to steal the Kremlin. Heh! What would the people think of this!" Even Salminsky is troubled, he retreats to the corner, turns his back to us and dials a number quick, says something fast in Russian.

"What? What did you do?" shouts Kirsanov, grabbing him around the neck. "Who did you call?"

"Nobody, just checking the market." He stands there, his arms above his head, a silly, servile smile dancing uncertainly on his face.

"Alpha troops. That's right. Fucking Jew."

"I've got our Streltsi. They'll grind your boys into the mud."

He whirls around to Zara Wonder, and motions her to a side room – just the two of them.

"Stop" yells Salminsky. "Stop. It's over. It's all over."

minus six

When I emerge from the church at last, the sky above is cloudless, clear and powder-blue, the sun unrelenting in its glare. The vultures with their cameras and microphones have scattered, there's just an empty field beyond, a lonely tram trundling down the nearest street. "Ah!" I exclaim, "peace," and picking up a fistful of sand let it filter through my palm and fall back on the earth again. "You're coming?" asks Salminsky, gesturing at his Mercedes.

"Sure," I answer, distractedly, when Kirk appears out of nowhere, comes running up to me breathless. "It's over," he announces. "It's all over. They've just devalued the rouble. Most of the major banks are going to collapse. The stock market has shut down. It's a total rout." He's excited, his eyes glisten, hand movements are rapid. I've never seen him so alive before.

"Really!"

"Yes, really, I just heard it from the CNN crew. They've all rushed back to the office to file their stories."

I go slack, collapse on the floor of the *maidan*, head in my hands. "It's over," I repeat. I guess we should have sensed it in Kirsanov's behavior. He knew all along, was just playing out his part. I wait for the sorrow to hit, for the chest-beating to begin, but there's nothing. Just the sound of distant traffic and Kirk's rapid breathing above. Nada. I stand up slowly after a while and turn to gaze at the church; its modest domes, their colors fading, seem to reproach me. "Vapshe," I mumble. "Vapshe huina."

Salminsky comes up to me. "You're coming?" he asks.

"I don't know." His features are distorted, his lips trembling, hands balled into fists.

"You know?"

"I just found out. They called me." He stamps his foot on the ground. "That bastard Kirsanov." He checks his watch. "There's still a few minutes before the banks close. I must go there and see if anything can be done."

"You're coming?"

I wave at him. "I'll just wander for a while. I need to think."

Kirk comes up to me again. "I'll walk with you. I feel like hanging out for a while."

"Don't you have to file?"

"Naw, there's others who cover business. I filed this story over the phone." He points at his cheap, plastic-encased Motorola proudly.

I just shrug and start walking towards the street. Prospekt Vernadskogo is a few blocks down, and then ... then. Then whatever.

"It's the end of an era. Russia's going to be forced to become a normal country after this. For a while everyone partied like there was no tomorrow. All these fortunes were made, mansions were bought in Mayfair and the South of France. Where was the money coming from? All the industries in the rust belt were bankrupt but billions of dollars were flowing out of

Russia. The government was just borrowing money to fund its war in Chechnya. It was a huge pyramid scheme. And now it's come crashing down like a house of cards."

I grab him around the neck. "Shut up. Just be quiet for a while. I need some time to think."

He gives me a strange look and then keeps silent, furrowing his brows, whistling a Beatles tune to himself. So we slog on through the heat. Near a metro I see a Caucasian women selling some chebyreks from a cloth-covered aluminum bucket. "Chebyreks, hot chebyreks," she shouts, but the pedestrians ignore her, shoot her covert glances, and then walk on fast, their hands on their pockets. I walk up to her.

"How much?"

"Ten roubles," she says sly.

"Ten roubles! That's almost two dollars."

She fans her face with a tin plate. "Devaluatse. Everything's more expensive."

So I hand her the ten roubles and walk on, biting into the chebyrek's rump, the meat soft and chewy there. Mmmm... We pass a Stolichny Bank, a crowd jostles outside, swearing and shouting, while two uniformed guards, their hands on their holsters, keep them at bay.

"Geez," whistles Kirk, "I guess their savings are going to be wiped out again. I'm lucky I never banked here."

A little kid in a fire-engine-red jumpsuit, snot congealed on his nose, pulls at his mother's arm while she gives me a lascivious look. "Mama, mama," he cries, but she ignores him, turns to smile at me from under her ridiculous sun hat. Her hair's stringy, sunflower blonde, her long tanned legs visible up to her thighs. Must have just returned from the Crimea, I think, and give her a quick wave before turning a corner. Other than that the streets are empty, eerie almost. We walk past long avenues where there's not a soul in sight; an old man spits out of a third-floor window and then coughs loudly. A few stray dogs bark at us and then slink away.

We're still in the south, far from the Kremlin, all these panel houses built by Kruschev—cheap wallpaper inside, the windows broken and boarded up with cardboard—line the road. Occasionally there's a courtyard and we peek in; a babushka swabs the cracked cement floor. There's a slight breeze, the birch trees rustle, some newspaper slides about, she looks up, sees us, and then turns back to her task without acknowledging our presence.

"Old lady," I ask, "do you know that your roubles are devalued, worthless."

"A peasant only crosses himself when thunder strikes," she mumbles, and hides her face with her scarf.

"Let's take a cab," I say suddenly. "This feels like the Bronx."

"Where to?"

"To the Sports Bar," I say on an impulse. "I haven't been there in years. Is it still around?"

"Yeah, it's still there. They have new management, I think. Chechens. Kicked out the foreigners who first opened it."

"Typical story. Russians invite the Westerners and then force them out after a while. Watch what'll happen in the next few months. You'll all be gone soon. Even you."

He laughs, sticks his head of out the cab and yodels, carefree. I've never seen him like this. "Journalists are vultures. The worse things get the more work we have. It's a great profession during a depression."

"But you depend on advertising."

He shakes his head and sings another tune. "That's just the Moscow Times. If this thing blows up, I could be writing for a hundred publications in America. It'll be like the good old days, when we were the white gods."

"You're twisted, really perverse."

But he just laughs again, his teeth as white as the wallpaper in his bourgeois apartment.

The Sports Bar is just as I remembered it, the waitresses in bobby sox, the television sets showing some baseball game. It's more built-up inside, though: there's a spray-painted Chevrolet pushed behind the pool table and some wire mesh over the dance floor. It seems seedier, the chrome bar dull and scratched in parts. So early 90s, I think. There's almost no-one around; it's six on a Friday evening, but the bar feels like a morgue. A few drunk Germans in a corner, oil workers perhaps, keep toasting themselves, their eyes bleary. Proust. Proust. And then again Proust.

We start to drink. Heinekens like the first time. "The menu still has the old rouble prices," exults Kirk. "It's gotten 50 percent cheaper in a single afternoon. Oh, I love this country."

The drunker I get, the more animated and alert is Kirk. I should have noticed that he was watching me intently, waiting for an opening, but I didn't. I was lost in my own thoughts. "It was because of you that I left Russia that time," I tell him after a while.

"Really!" He screws his eyes together, rests his glance on the Om pendant. He doesn't believe me, of course. It's Russia's fault. We've lived in a speeded-up world these past few years, the time machine cranked into the red zone. Things which took decades in the West happened here in a few months. We went from idealistic flower-power children of the 60s in perestroika days to cocaine-snorting yuppies in a few years. I remember the summer of '97 when rock bands were shoved to the outer edges of Moscow by rave music, which mutated by fall into Berlin techno—which was soon incorporated into Russian pop with DJ Groove and others. Neither he nor I can remember the Godunev who worked days at the kiosk with those smoldering eyes of his, his head in the clouds. "It was so long ago, so fucking long ago," I say, banging the beer stein on the table. "It seems as far away as the Roman Empire."

"It's going to be back," he says. "The old days, sitting around the kitchen table drinking vodka, eating tushonka from cans with black bread."

"Perhaps you're right." Perhaps you're right, I repeat, perhaps you're right, perhaps you're right. I scoot downstairs for no reason, enter the bathrooms, and sit on the toilet seat, waiting to take a dump. I'm not sure I want to shit but I know that I must. Soon enough it comes, rushing through the rectum, viscous and gaseous. Aahh! When it's done I feel so good I want to dance. I return to the bar and stand up on the table and do a little twist. I feel so good, so good, I croon as James Brown might. It's all over, I think, the New Russian fascism, the tyranny of hedonism. I twist some more, watching the waiter, an Indian, pick his nose with his finger and then take it out again quickly, glancing over coyly to see if I've noticed him. I can see again, I exult. I can see. I can see that the Yank is still a bit afraid of me, self-conscious in my presence; I bend down and twist his cheek. "White god! Where's the powder?"

A waitress comes running up to us. "New menu," she says, slamming it on the table.

"But we ordered from the old menu. We pay the old rouble prices, don't we?"

She puts her hand on her hips. "I have to ask the manager. I'll be back."

When I sit down again, he leans forward. "How come you gave me that scoop last night? How did you know it was going to happen?"

"Oh that." I wave a hand in the air as if it had happened years ago. With the rouble collapse it does seem like another era. "We planned the whole thing."

His eyes widen, he leans over, his breath smelling of beer and adrenaline.

"Tell me about it."

So I tell him, the whole story, the privatization of the Kremlin, the Zara Wonder plan, the madness of Kirsanov. What did it matter, I think. It's all over now. It feels great confiding in a white person, someone who sees it all from the outside. Yes, we were mad I admit, we thought we could do anything. And I guess we might have if all this hadn't happened.

He sits there still while I blab, earnest, adding phrases here and there, whistling with surprise at times. "I even kissed her," I add at last. "Kissed her vomit. Stripped of her entourage and her lawyers and all that she was like any other scared person. The KGB could have broken her down in a day had they wanted to. Americans are weak, that's all. They've got this big aura of success and glamour, but poke them a bit, and their bubble bursts." I laugh insanely, so loud and mad that even the sozzled Germans turn to stare at us. "Even gave her some coke. She snorted it up through that haughty WASP nose of hers."

He's so excited he starts to sweat. "Who else was involved in this?" he asks, leaning forward, almost panting.

I'm suspicious for a second, his questions are a bit too probing. "You're not going to write an article about this, are you?"

He turns crimson, takes a big swig of beer. "Of course not. We're friends, aren't we? I still owe you a big one for Masha. She's the greatest." He shakes his head. "Noboby would believe me anyway. It's too outrageous, even for Russia."

I'm so drunk I believe him. "I'm just suspicious, that's all."

But the mood's spoiled. He's broken it with his nosy questions. I don't want to talk any more. I want to do something very quiet, curl up in bed and read some Pushkin. Wait till it's darker and watch the stars. I'm a changed person, I decide. I'll take up painting, retire to some estate in Montana, and capture the colors of the rugged landscape on canvas.

"I'm going," I say. "See you later." And I just walk out of there, sticking him with the bill. Walking down the Arbat trying to hail a cab, I'm so thirsty I stop into the nearest kiosk for some mineral water. There's two bottles of Dobraya Voda water on the cabinet behind the salesman.

"How much?"

"Twenty roubles."

"How about the other? There's a tag saying ten roubles."

"Oh, that's from the pre-devaluation stock. You can have it for ten."

"And that one?"

"That came in this afternoon. It's more expensive."

So I buy the ten-rouble water and walk out of there. "You're ancient," I tell it, holding it up before my face. "You belong to the past. Perhaps if I drink you I'll go back to this spring. Just like Alice in Wonderland." I take a big swig, some water spills on my jacket; I take another, wait for something to happen. Nothing. I gulp some more down and wait. Nothing again, just a Pravda newspaper which flies up from somewhere and lands at my feet. I pick it up and flip the pages idly when a car screeches to a halt on the Arbat. "Bastard, raper of Russia," screams someone and starts shooting. Rat-tat-tat. Merciless. I dodge and run behind the kiosk, shivering there like a coward. The bottle's been hit, though, water trickles out and washes off the summer dust from my scuffed Hugo Boss loafers.

minus three

Another Aeroflot flight out of Russia. This time first-class. I'd still got some dollars stuffed under the mattress, never went for the bank scams as the others did. There's also a stewardess from Siberia this time but her butt isn't as hard as that first one. I'm not horny either, just want to get drunk on those mini bottles of white Chablis and stretch out my legs. "Da," I go, "Da, vapshe huina," after the fifth bottle of wine, and recline the seat, lean back, so that the cool air from the fan above caresses my unshaven face.

It's been so frenetic these last few weeks since the crash that I haven't had time to think. Been running from one friend's apartment to the next to escape those Georgian mafiosi. They're convinced that I—and Irina—were responsible for Chevchavadze's death, the slick Armani-clad businessman who handed her the rose because I flashed her breast at him. I think Salminsky has double-crossed us but it's hard to be sure. Did he?

Wait. I lean back some more and savor the calm which pervades my mind now, thoughts as intimate as coke-induced conversations. They're like an E-type Jaguar with synchronized steering, I can guide them effortlessly with just a little shake of my head. It wasn't like that this past week: I was so frenetic I had no control over them. They came and went like soap bubbles, just as I tried to grab onto one it went pop, disappeared, to be replaced by another meaningless apparition.

Aeroflot. There's nothing like flying to concentrate the mind, give it power over its minions. The collapse of Russia, I think. It was an event, to be sure. Everyone I guess came out pretty well in the end except for poor Masha with her doe-like eyes, her unquestioning devotion to that traitor Kirk. She was killed outside the Jazz Kafe last night, strangled by Stalker the old-fashioned way, gloved hands pressed tight around her neck, in retribution for her boyfriend's back-stabbing. Kirsanov had ordered the killing; disgraced and out of favor, he craved one last act of retribution. Well, serves Kirk right. Despite his promises the snitch had written a front-page article in the Moscow Times about the attempt to privatize the Kremlin. It was headlined, "The Oligarchs' Last Stand: the Rape of the Kremlin," and described the scheme in great detail. He had gotten someone in the Kremlin's inner circle, a disgruntled friend of Kirsanov, to spill the beans. He had mentioned Salminsky, and Godunev of course, and the Richard Gere look-alike. Zara Wonder wasn't brought up, though. I guess he was right in that no-one would believe him, they'd think it was too outrageous. Yeltsin had ordered an investigation after the article appeared, a few heads had rolled, including the chief of the Privatization Agency and that of Kirsanov. He was getting out of hand anyway, it was a good excuse for the wily Yeltsin to give him the boot. The prosecutors had started investigating; Salminsky's offshore accounts were frozen on the order of the Russian government, but it would take them months, if not years, to get at the truth. That bastard Kirk. I think Salminsky would have finished him off without a second's thought if the

Western media hadn't started circling. CNN and all the rest had done a special on the supposed deal, even the Russian press had started sniffing around. Kirk had appeared on some of the major American TV shows, 60 Minutes and others; he was planning to write a book, I heard. His proximity to me, his attendance at the bashes, and now the murder of his girlfriend had given him a morbid cachet that the other hacks just didn't have. "He's going to be the next Hunter Thompson," Joe had remarked. Well, good for him. Perhaps he'll be a white god again.

Even Salminsky was as cheerful as ever, despite losing his entire fortune in that bungled deal. The resilience of us Russians! It amazes me sometimes. We almost crave adversity, sudden changes of fortune. It gives us the strength to keep on living. The last time I had seen him he was hiding out in some communal apartment near Chisty Prudy. He had come to the door shirtless, his hairy stomach hanging out over cheap dungarees, a scraggy beard covering his face. "Come in, come in," he had exclaimed, hugging me. "Let's drink some vodka together. Have you brought some?" he asked, his beady eyes searching me hungrily.

"Sure."

He was sharing a grungy Soviet-era flat with some grandmother, a common toilet in the hallway. His little room was a mess, books scattered everywhere, musty souvenirs from the Crimea and Yugoslavia lining the shelves. A cheap computer screen blinked on his desktop. He smelled of canned beef and Baltika beer. I don't think he had bathed in days. "I haven't left the apartment for two weeks," he confided. "They'll never find me here."

After a few shots, he was the same old Salminsky, rumba-ing around the apartment, that mad glint in his eyes. "I'm going back to graduate school," he declared. "Fermat's Theorem hasn't been solved yet, it was a hoax. I'm going to crack the code. I've spoken to Princeton, they're quite willing to have me back."

"What about the prosecution?"

He waved his hand in the air. "Oh, that. They'll blame the Americans, claim it was all some plot of the Clinton administration to destabilize the great Mother Russia." He lowered his voice. "The Georgians are the ones to worry about."

"I know," I said and mentioned the attempted contract killing on the Arbat.

"What about Arkady? Haven't heard from him a while."

He banged his hand on the rumpled bed where we're sitting. "He took the first flight out of Russia. Got scared shitless. Thought they'd arrest him for his involvement. These Americans, they can't handle adversity."

Then he had grown philosophical, gazed at the cracked cornice of the ceiling and squashed a fly between his chubby palms. "It's better this way, isn't it? We were all so mad, so desperate to project some hip image, living so much in the moment. How long was Caligula's reign? Just four years. The tyranny of the New Russia was even less, perhaps just three. And still it seems that it lasted forever. Now we'll go back to drinking vodka and reading our classics. And I'll tell you what, the vodka will taste better than the best Hennessy cognac." He motions at the wooden door of the room. "I have chats with my landlady, Natasha Solovnieva. Her husband was in the war, took part in the capture of Berlin from the Nazis. I'm going to help her write her memoirs." He shakes his head, kills another fly. "Those days, we'd have run her over if she crossed the street in front of our Mercedes. We all, as Mayakovsky said, had clouds in our trousers." He's getting more emotional as he drinks, tears spring out his eyes. "Godunev, you always wanted to maintain some inner purity. Don't think I didn't notice that. I understood that you never quite accepted our Russia even though you were part of it. You still have that money, you were smart. Get together with Irina, she's a wonderful girl, and move somewhere else. Paint for a while, forget all this madness. We'll meet again in a few years and open a bookstore somewhere. In Paris on the left bank. We'll have lots of cats, ocelots and Russian blues. And we'll be like the poets of the Silver Age, drinking smuggled absinthe from Spain."

When I'm leaving, I ask him if he needs some money. His ears prick up like a hungry dog's. "You still have some dollars?"

"Sure, I hid them under the mattress."

"Oh, I don't need any," he says quickly, and turns away embarrassed. "I have some old roubles left. A few thousand. And some furniture. The pool table also. Someone stole the Mercedes."

I take out five hundred dollars and give it to him. He presses them into his palm stealthily and stands up to hug me. "You really are the incarnation of Prince Myshkin. God bless you." And he crosses himself in the Orthodox way. The first time I had seen him do that.

He was right, of course. It was a wonderful time after the rouble collapsed. We all discovered our Russianness again, experienced a collective guilt about having spurned it so easily for the materialism of the West. Even the trendiest bars banned Western alcohol and served cheap Belarussian vodka for a dollar a shot. Since there were no imported goods in the stores, their shelves were empty, we all went back to eating canned sardines with black bread and Ukrainian butter. We'd sit around for hours in someone's apartment, talking again for the first time it seemed. Having intense conversations about the poets, our inner nature, the transience of the soul. Back to the past. It was all a bit giddy, we were grown adults discovering the forgotten pleasures of our childhood again. We reminisced about the past as we hadn't in years; in the mid-90s it had been taboo to discuss the Soviet times. The present had been such an egomaniac, it had strangled the past. Now the past revived again, in spurts and gasps, bringing with it the colors and smells of the old regime. They weren't all that bad. "The Soviet times were OK," people said again and again. "At least we had soul."

Ex-New Russians unloaded their Mercedes and BMWs for a couple thousand dollars and retired to their dachas. Some of them bought Pobedas and Volgas from the Stalinist era, fixing them up and transforming them into convertibles. Funkiness was back. Some young girls dressed in their grandmothers' clothes to make a statement; the men wore fake Levis and cheap denim for the hell of it. The foreigners with their fat expense accounts were all heading for the exits and we'd attend their farewell parties for the free booze and food. Richard Gere left in a hurry, the Russians expelled him for his role in the accident. They wanted to show the West they took the incident seriously.

He had a nostalgic farewell party in his flash apartment in one of the Stalin towers. It was crammed with young girls, his ex-girlfriends, their friends, the models from Red Star I invited along, strippers from Rasputin; all polishing off his drinks cabinet, guzzling his alcohol greedily. I had never seen him so pathetic. He just hung back in the kitchen and gaped at the girls. "It's all over," he kept saying. "It's all fucking over. I'm going to have to go back to the West and get a normal job as a banker. I'll never have so much fun again. I'm 28 years old and I feel that the best days of my life are over. Can you understand that?"

A girl comes up to him. "You kiss me softly in the dark and leave me in the quiet. There will not be in your window a golden bird again." His eyes become moist. "Godunev," he cries. "How can I leave?"

"Have a good time at least," I order, and drag them both into his bedroom. When he emerges a while later, he's happier. "I'm going to write a screenplay. I have decided to take a year off and just write. It'll make a wonderful movie won't it, the past few years."

I kiss him on the lips. I'm beginning to like the guy even though I sealed his fate. "There's a poet inside even you. I'd never have guessed. Crises open the eyes of men.

"I'll give you some advice. Take back a girl with you, any one of them. They're all desperate to leave now. You won't regret it."

Last I heard he did bring back a Lyuba with him to New York. She's studying fashion at FIT and he's writing a screenplay as he promised.

Joe was expelled also as a matter of course. But he snuck back in through Belarus. He was expelled again but went to Lithuania and bought himself a passport for $10,000 and returned. He bribed the officials at the Ministry of Foreign Affairs with teenage girls so they relented at last. He had a big bash to celebrate. "I'll never leave, Godunev," he said. "I'm going to die here like John Reed and be buried on Red Square." He was one of those foreigners who can't live outside Russia, they wither like Draculas in the bright sun of the West.

I'd have stayed on in Russia, retired to the Altai mountains and painted for a while if the Georgians hadn't been after me. They were relentless, they didn't forget and forgive as we Russians did. They were convinced that I had played a part in his murder, (why, I still don't understand) and now that we were weak, they had decided to strike. I asked Salminsky to intervene and he did, he claimed, but it didn't help.

They tried again once, rigged my BMW with an explosive device. The driver was killed. So at last I bought a fake passport (the Russian government would never have allowed me to leave), finagled a visa from the Americans and bought the ticket. So here I am. There's just Irina to deal with now. Even the twins have gone, left for Germany, where they want to become MTV stars. Olga called me once from somewhere, Essen I think. "Where's my icon?" she asked. "It got stuck in customs," I said. "They're going to arrest Andrei Rublyev."

"It doesn't matter. Come here, there's lots of parties."

"Later perhaps."

First I want to kill Irina. The Georgians will get her anyway, they've vowed to avenge their man's death. They traced the offshore company and found she was the owner, so they think she had a part also. It's better, I reason, that she dies at my hands than under the gun of some Caucasian bandit. Plus I think I hate her. She's like a cancerous cell, I think; if it weren't for her treason, and her tempting me with those dollars, none of this would have happened. I'd have escaped the original sin. In absentia, I blame her for the intellectual vacuity of the New Russia. It was girls like her, with their provincial opportunism, their amoral character, and complete indifference to art, which made it all happen. All they wanted was to be a bit more fashionable than their classmates, a bit more avant-garde, so their mothers back home might be proud of them. She was as fickle as the wind, Irina, with Kirk when Americans were trendy back then, and then part of our *tusovka* when the Russians took over the scene.

There's a gun waiting for me at the airport, one of my old Brighton Beach contacts. I'll shoot her after forcing her to sign our joint account over to me. I can't deny that money is part of the motive, I want that cash to myself so I can retire somewhere, forget all this madness. But I push that to the back of my mind, think of her blank face at the Pushkin instead, her complete lack of comprehension when I swooned before a Bonnard.

Another chablis and I unlace my shoes, sit there in socks, watch the in-flight movie lazily for a while. Then I open the letter from Zara Wonder. She thanks me for my help in Moscow, invites me to visit her in her French-style gated chateau in Beverly Hills. There's a touch of romance in the letter, a hint that she might be willing to take me on as her lover. I think had I not kissed her then she would not have been able to walk out of there with her head held high. "I do not want you to think that I exploited your feelings for me in any sense. They were, to some extent, during that most stressful time in my life, mutual." The letter is signed, "The pretty girl on the bicycle." She remembers that I mentioned her early role in Goodbye Evenings. Perhaps I'll visit her. Hang around Hollywood for a while. Why not?

I yawn, cover myself with a red blanket, push my head against a scented white pillow, and drift off into dreamland. I haven't slept so well in weeks.

the end of zero

The door opens. The man in front of me looks weird, cartoonish, with his wide, sheepish eyes and unnatural muscles which don't fit his geeky face at all. It's all happening too fast, crazier than I imagined. I advance towards him and he backs off, even though he's twice my size.

"It's all a misunder.. mistanding," he stammers.

"Do you know who I am?" I ask, coming close and pushing my face against his. "I Russia mafia and I kill you, you bastard. That's my girlfriend there."

He puts his hands in front of his face. "Let's juu..juust talk. It's the cocaine, I've never done it before."

His eyes swivelled over to the barrel of my pistol. "Hey," he mouths, I pull the trigger. Bang. I shake my head.

"It is blank. Russian roulette. Next time better," and he scuttles through the door.

Irina throws herself at me, sobbing, hysterical; a white sheet wrapped around her. "Oh Godunev, it's you. I can't believe this, I didn't trust my eyes." Then she drags me quickly into the apartment.

I'm disappointed that I'm still somewhat jealous.

"Who's that?"

"Oh, him!" She shrugs. "You know all that happened today-with the murder in Moscow. I just brought him along as a bodyguard, just in case." She hugs me from behind, kisses me on the back of the neck.

"Godunishka, I had a feeling you'd come. Oh, I love Russians. I love Russians," she coos, before throwing herself at me hysterically.

"What's going on, Godunev? They announced on television that I was murdered in Moscow. Who's behind all this? I called Salminsky but his number's not picking up. I even called you..." She closes her eyes shy. "But then I hung up."

"Yes, I remember getting a call when I had just arrived at JFK. I thought it might be you." I turn grave, hold her hand in mine, simpatico. "It's the Georgians. They're after all of us."

"The Georgians! But what have I done?" She widens her eyes and then gestures about the room as if proof of the crime might be found here. She's changed quite a bit since Moscow: her hair's blond now and cropped short, falls in bangs over her eyes. It turns her features sharper, emphasizes the flare of her nostrils and the fullness of her lips; gives her face a strength it lacked before. The sweetness of her youth is still there when she gazes at me lovingly, but it disappears when she turns away to stare out the windows at Manhattan in the night. A stranger would find her intimidating, sphinx-like. Bitchy.

"It's all about that murder we witnessed." I bring her up to date with their discovery of the owner of the Alphabeta company, and their attempts to murder both me and Salminsky. "When the cat is away, the mice play." I don't mention Kirk's betrayal, or my part in having Masha's murder miscontrued as hers. (I had told the police when they brought me to the crime scene that it was Ira. At the time I had wanted to play a small joke, prepare the ground for my visit.) It doesn't seem necessary.

"Boze Moi, oh my God," she cries, covering her face in her hands. She starts to sob again—silent, snuffled tears. "Who was killed, anyway?"

I wave a hand in the air. "Masha. Kirk's girl."

"Masha!" She gives me a surprised look.

"Kirk's girl. You saw her at parties with him. They thought she was you."

"Masha." She rolls her eyes back in an effort to remember. "That quiet girl, who always seemed so lonely. She used to hide behind him at parties. Poor thing." She pretends to grieve but the killing appeals to her vanity. It tickles her, I can tell, that someone died on her account. She's like me in a sense—we've both got this preternatural cruel streak.

I feel awkward. I've come to kill her and now I'm cast in the role of her protector. The bonds which held us together in the past strain at me again now. There's a level of comfort there I realize, a naturalness I hadn't appreciated before. I feel like I could vomit on her crystal table top and it wouldn't mean a thing. I stand up and pace about her apartment. I don't want to sit in front of her so she can work her feminine charms.

"It's like a bordello," I declaim. "There's nothing here except for a huge TV and a black leather couch. What kind of life are you leading? Where are the books?"

"Coke?" she asks. "I've got some fantastic Venezuelan. The coke here cannot be compared with the shit we got in Moscow."

So we sit there and hoover up the pinkish lines from her table top with a hundred-rouble bill I've still got left in my wallet. Devil's dandruff makes me vulnerable, I have a tendency to get introspective, talk about myself too much. But this stuff is different, it gets me so high I'm content to just sit there and watch her watch me.

She's still wrapped in her sheet, but she throws it off and sits there naked. There's a mermaid tattoo on her navel that I hadn't seen before. She smiles at me, closes her eyes, and runs a sensuous hand down her neck.

"With you I feel so relaxed. I know nothing's going to happen tonight at least."

I shift in my seat uncomfortably. I can't allow myself to get nostalgic about us.

"What's New York like?" I ask instead.

She gestures around the apartment. "This is New York. This is what it's given me. A nice apartment and a comfortable life. Life is easy here. If you're beautiful," she gestures at herself, "you can get lots of work. Mostly catalogue stuff, some editorials. But Russian girls are hot these days. We're in demand."

She fluffs her hair about, prims her face. "But otherwise it sucks. Americans are not people, they're robots. Everyone is so career-oriented here, focused on their work, doing long hours at the office or wherever. They absolutely don't know how to have a good time. They can't be spontaneous at all. Everything is planned weeks in advance and it's all so predictable. Launch party here, art opening there, fashion show at Bryant Park. It's the same shit, no-one has a good time. They drink a few cocktails, get just a bit drunk, and then head home before any madness can start."

She stands up and does a Jazz Kafe vogue, moving her hands in sync with her hips. "You remember those parties we used to have. I would give everything right now for one night back in Moscow. Where I could just be crazy, get high and scream my lungs out."

"People here respect beautiful women too much. They're so careful around us, so polite, it drives me mad. They all want sex, these Americans, they're obsessed with it. But they're also ashamed of wanting it. They're like boys, the men never grow up. They're making strange jokes all the time about some TV show, or getting all excited about an obscure artist. Or baseball game. And all this race stuff between blacks and whites. It's just too complicated."

She catches my eye, and then averts her gaze when a light blush spreads across her cheeks. "There're some Italians boys around. They're OK."

She sticks her tongue out at me. "But seriously, this place sucks. It's like ancient Athens or something like that. Remember those stories we read in school about Socrates and Plato, sitting around and philosophizing all the time. Not doing anything. That's how these New Yorkers are. We Russians are like the Romans, action, lights, aggression. Want to live life to the fullest, cultivate our sensual side. Our poets, our bodies, our nature. We were called the Third Rome, weren't we?" she asks, standing before me like a schoolgirl.

"You didn't talk like this before. What's happened to you?"

She shakes her head in the air, makes a motion of jabbing me in the chest.

"You underestimated me, Godunev. You thought I was just another bimbo. That's because in Russia pretty girls must act silly, so I went along. Perhaps a bit too much." She stretches her hands out in the air. "Here I feel so free. I can express any opinion, no matter how stupid, and they'll take me seriously. And of course I have all these guys take me out to dinner and talk a lot of nonsense to impress me, so I learn something here and there."

She makes as if to bite me. "You'll have a hard time here. Girls will think you're too slick, or that you're sleazy. Better you stay with me and save your ego."

I crook my finger in the air. "Come here, come here, you soothsayer. You have changed, haven't you?"

When she comes to me, I bite her playfully on her clavicle and make to kiss her. "Kiss me, not the frogs," I say. (It's an old joke between us, frogs a reference to some Frenchies she hung around with when we first met.) She laughs, puts an arm around me, bends her face forwards, and is about to meet my lips, when her expression darkens suddenly. She jerks her head back and narrows her eyes.

"You bastard. Remember that last time. You almost raped me and threw me out of OUR apartment. That was just two days before I was leaving for New York. And you haven't called even once since then to apologize." She sticks her thumb at the bathroom. "If it weren't for what went down today, I'd never have welcomed you like this. But still … you're an asshole."

She untangles herself from me and stands up. Pokes me in the ribs. "What do you want, eh? Russia collapses so you come here. To New York. Now that you're no longer the big cheese, you remember Irina. Sweet Irina, the one you fucked when she was sixteen. Confused, lost, stupid Irina. We've got some money together, you even thought. You fucker. I hate Russian men." She goes up to the mantelpiece of her fireplace, and, picking up a picture, smashes it against the granite floor. "I had that picture of us in Salminsky's dacha up there. Just for the men who came here, so I could pretend I had a Russian boyfriend. But fuck you." She kicks the glass shards with her bare feet and then stamps the cardboard frame. She gestures at the front door. "I'd kick you out right now, but since you're here to protect me, I'll let you stay a while. Don't accuse me of being ungrateful."

She breaks into sobs, covers her face with her hands.

"Things were going almost well here. OK, New York's a bit too self-righteous for me, but I was getting settled. I was making a career, I was even dating someone." She waves her hand dismissively when I look at her questioningly. "He's in Italy right now. But it doesn't matter. Things were OK until this morning. Then I hear about this murder, and then you show up. Like the Grim Reaper. A ghost from the past, so that I get all shaken up. I had almost forgotten Moscow, its craziness. And the way I was then, trying so hard to fit in with the crowd. Not that you noticed. You were too busy being cool, impassive, to feel anything, to notice anything. And when you were drunk, you went for the cheap whores who couldn't challenge you. Don't think I didn't know. I just didn't say anything because it was none of my business. And I'm not the jealous type." Her chest is heaving, she stumbles backwards and falls against the couch. Beads of sweat appear on her brow.

"Tell me I'm wrong if you like. But first explain what you're doing here. Why did you come to see me again? To apologize or just to use me again as you used to?"

I clench my teeth, my jaws grinding because of the coke. She's turned into a David Lynch girl, vengeful and mean-spirited. I can't stand her again.

I cross my arms and announce matter-of-fact.

"I came here to kill you."

She sticks her jaw out. "Oh yeah! Well, kill me then. Go ahead, blow my brains out. I'm already dead as far as everyone else is concerned."

"OK," I say, very calm. I pick up the gun from the table and walk towards her, putting the barrel against her temple. "I'll just shoot right now, if you don't mind."

"Go ahead," she says. "Go right ahead, you bastard. You'll be doing me a favor. You'll also be doing THEM a favor. They set you up, don't you realize that, Salminsky, Arkady, the whole gang. Turned you into the fall guy, the one they could blame when things went wrong, like now."

I hit her forehead lightly with the barrel of the gun. "Shut up. Don't try to seduce me with lies."

She closes her eyes and grows very still, not even breathing. Her face goes blank as a slate, devoid of emotion. Then it clouds up again and something rises to the surface; her face turns compassionate, is suffused with pity. Almost as if she were Jesus Christ mourning for mankind. I've never seen such a pure emotion before; perhaps once, outside a church in Orenburg, an old woman mourning our tragedy in space. But that was a long, long time ago.

I whisper quietly. "Irina, Irina, are you there?" But she doesn't respond. Even though her eyes are closed, I can see the pupils roll upwards to the back of her head. She gets even stiller, her face cold to the touch, and then she begins to tremble slightly, her flat stomach vibrating just so, like a Japanese washing machine. Her legs twitch, one eyelid flutters. She seems to be entering some sort of trance—I've never seen her like this before.

The gun shakes in my hand. "Irina," I scream. "Wake up, wake up. I'm sorry." I shake her mad as if she were dead already. "Oi, my heart," she moans, opening her eyes. I collapse in front of her, put my head on her knees. "Irina."

"What?"

"It's also your fault," I whisper. "You were Eve, I hate the Bible and stuff. But if you hadn't tempted me with the half a million dollars, I wouldn't have got so tight with Salminsky. And you deceived me about going to Riga once a month, lying that it was Saratov instead."

"We had just met Godunev. I had a whole life in Moscow before you arrived. Russian girls are supposed to be mysterious anyway. Men don't respect them if they confide in everything. You wouldn't have appreciated me if I had told you everything I had done in the past." We're both whispering at each other. I don't know why.

"Oh," I say, "you were just so vapid and vain. You never saw that I never quite fit into the scene and that I wanted something more from life than just going to the parties and acting glamorous. You just wanted to be the party girl, and impress others by being with the right guy."

"You really think so?" She nudges me playfully in the neck. "That night I met you, you were a nobody. You had just arrived from America with some cheap 30th-street suitcases and a few hundred dollars. That's all. Don't forget that."

"I can't explain everything. I just want to forget everything, that's all. You're the last person from the past who still chains me down. I just want to be free again, as I was back in the days when I worked at the kiosk."

She leans forwards and runs her cold hands along my face.

"Let's just go to a club. What's the hottest club in New York these days?" But my voice lacks conviction and she realizes that. Sees that I'm weak for once. She sings an old folk song, Katinka instead, and even I whistle along with the tune.

"You're always running away, aren't you, Godunev?" she says, still caressing me soft with her hands. "You ran away from Moscow when things got uncomfortable at first. And before that, you escaped Orenburg or wherever you grew up to come to Moscow. And then you left America in a huff, flew back to Moskva. There you became *kruta*, a trend-setter, but still you're not happy. You have to leave when the crisis hits. The Georgians you say, but you could have dealt with that. Dealt with the others. What's wrong with you, Godunichka? Why are you afraid of feeling, of getting involved? Why do you always want to be outside, disengaged?" She pulls at my hair. "You think you're Lermentov's Pecchorin, don't you. As cynical and heartless as the Caucasian mountains. Perhaps when you were younger it was OK. But you're getting older, almost 30 now, how long can you keep running away? Where are you going to go now?"

"To Hollywood. Zara Wonder invited me. I might get into the movie business."

"Right. You'll hang around there for a while, turn into a successful party promoter, like that Fellacio character. Then you'll have a disastrous affair with some actress or someone will punch you in the face at a drunken premiere and you'll leave. Drive into Mexico. Until one day you'll end up in Tierra del Fuego, the loneliest man on earth."

"Stop it. Stop it."

"Stop it. You're listening to me for the first time ever." She picks up the gun and presses its barrel against my temple. "Why don't I shoot you instead? Put you out of your misery."

"Shoot," I intone calmly. "Shoot if you want to."

She jerks the gun against me for a bit, makes a motion of pulling the trigger. And then stops sudden. "I love you Godunev," she says, very quiet. "I've always loved you. Didn't you ever notice?"

I do something very stupid then. I start to cry. I haven't cried in years, not since those kids put a frog under my chair in school. Once or twice since then when I was high on vodka. But not like this. So open it embarrasses me. First I cry, then I break into sobs, pushing my mouth against her hands. It's so pathetic, this outburst of emotion, that I cry even more, just depressed at the pathos of it all. I can't stop even though I try. Every sob or two, I imagine it'll turn into laughter, but it doesn't. It just goes on and on, like the wind in the trees outside our Moscow apartment on fall nights. "Godunev, Godunev," she goes, wiping off my tears with the back of her hands.

"Let it all out. Just let it out, the pain, the sorrow. You can't hold it bottled up for so long."

So I succumb to the suppressed need inside me, just bawl unashamedly, like I'm at a funeral. I cry for Masha, for the friends who might have doublecrossed me, for Russia itself, for a lost and pristine youth. It's all gone, I think, and I'm so sad about it, I realize. Never realized until now that I loved those years in Moscow so much. The mad parties, that feeling of absolute control. The sense that everything was possible, that the world could give a damn. That we were living everything for the first time, writing the book of life itself. Everything so new, so exciting sometimes. And we thought it would go on for ever and ever. I think of Salminsky in those scruffy dungarees, unshaven, drinking tea from a chipped ceramic cup in that miserable apartment of his. Expecting a knock on his door at any minute, but still brave, planning a new future. I think of those late-night kitchen parties after the rouble collapsed, Camilla in her blond pigtails sitting in a corner, so overjoyed now that Russia had found its soul again. Boze Moi. Here I am, in ancient Athens, where everything has been done and explored, sitting in a cold apartment with a girl who loves me. And there's nowhere else to go. I have no more energy left, it's all been pissed away in the nights.

"Let's go," she says kind. She drags me into the bedroom, to her four-poster bed, its headboard inlaid with mirrors, and sets me down. We both lie there quietly for a while. And then we have sex. It's very slow, intimate, pauses for conversation in between; nothing like the stud sex of the past. It goes on for a long, long time because of the cocaine. After I come, I just lay there for an eternity on top of her, massaging her ears and underarms. Then we smoke cigarettes (she still has Parliament Lights) and lie side by side. It's like our second night together, after that insane day spent chasing a high.

"We can go Buenos Aires," she says. "I hear South America is fantastic. It's a great city with tango music and outrageous style. Argentinians are like Russians, just as confused and flamboyant. Tasty beef, and strong wine. I'll study design there. After working with all these incompetent designers, I want to become one myself. It's more intellectual work than being a model."

"I'll paint. I'll just spend days like Van Gogh, wandering about the city, setting an easel down on a quiet street and streaking color on the canvas. I'll paint like the impressionists. But so what? I'm not doing it to be avant-garde." Strange. I don't feel this need to twist my thoughts, to render them enigmatic and unintelligable. I just spit them out as soon as they congeal in my mind. I must be getting old I think. That's what it is. I'm turning into an old fart.

She hugs me tight against her. "The Georgians will never find us there. They've probably never heard of Argentina."

"The Georgians? Is it true what you said about Salminsky, that they used me as a fall guy, exploited me."

She presses my sweaty hand in hers, brings it to her lips, speaks through it. "Yes, I knew about it, and wanted to warn you, but you left me before I could. You were so visible, an easy target for retribution later, if need be." She kisses my hand, scrapes her tongue against the rise on my palm. "It's too late now. Don't even think about it."

She sits up straight on the bed. "My heart," she says, putting a finger on her chest, "It's beating so fast, from the coke and all the excitement of the day." She rolls her eyes. "I guess all the sex hasn't helped either."

The old Godunev can't resist rearing his head. "Stop being so dramatic. It'll be the same old shit in the morning."

"No, Godunev, no," she cries, grabbing me around the buns. "Don't be so passive, like the Russians. We'll be different this time. It won't be like the past. I've changed, I won't allow it."

"You're like an American girl now."

"So what? Do you want some pliant Russian dyevooska? What do you want?"

I feel my mother's spirit strong in the room and can't breathe as I try to articulate an unfamiliar urge inside. "An artist," I whisper finally. "A real artist. One who creates things that mean something after everyone's dead. That's what I want, Ira."

Sentimental, I hold her tight as my thoughts are drowned out in the flutter of her fast-beating heart.

"Kiss me, Irr, not the frogs."

www.ingramcontent.com/pod-product-compliance
Lightning Source LLC
LaVergne TN
LVHW051554070426
835507LV00021B/2570